MW00907076

Daddy,
Your Shoes Didn't
Fit My Feet

Fred Holbrook

Dedication

This book is dedicated to my precious and loving wife, Lynn. She has been with me for over fifty years, working with and supporting me through the good times and the bad. I would never have gotten here without her help. Thank you, sweetheart, for your belief and trust in me.

We owe much to family and friends. They have been such an encouragement to Lynn and me. We realize we don't have room to mention everyone, but we do want to honor Chuck and Kate Kinney. What a blessing and support they have been to us through the years. Thank you, Chuck and Kate.

Acknowledgements

I especially want to acknowledge Pastor Tom and Millie Hepworth, who are now with the Lord, for all their sound advice and good years of teaching at Elma Bible Chapel in Elma, Washington.

I also want to thank Pastor Dale and Marianne Ray of Lakeview Community Church, Lk. Havasu City, Az., for your great leadership, your powerful messages, and for being good friends.

I would also like to acknowledge all of my friends and family who have encouraged me into finishing this book.

Forward

It has been my distinct privilege to know Fred Holbrook and his wife Lynn for over 20 years. I treasure their friendship and have found them to be people of their word and generous in every way.

I am also thankful to have been their Pastor and for their service as Elders at Lakeview Community Church in Lake Havasu City, Arizona. I appreciate their ability to teach, mentor, and to pray as spiritual warriors.

Through the years I have heard bits and pieces of Fred's life story. I have enjoyed the adventures of a back-woods boy and my heart has responded with deep appreciation of God's saving Grace as Fred shared his life's challenges of how God brought him through. I am thrilled to know that Fred's memories are recorded and that God is truly bigger than our problems.

Pastor Dale Ray

****

The life story of Fred Holbrook is an unforgettable journey that will inspire you to rise above mountain-like obstacles that may face you. From the path of unstable beginnings to the unshakeable knowledge of his Creator, this honest account of his life's struggles to find acceptance and peace of mind is an encouragement to never give up. Knowing Fred today I marvel at the transition that can occur when the touch of God is upon an individual. He has not only been a good friend to me but a role model that is worth following. Everyone that reads this book will receive a breath of fresh air in a world that is polluted with unhappy endings. You will enjoy his down to earth style of writing that reveals the person that he is...down to earth. Enjoy the journey!

Pastor Joe Grochocki
"The Gathering Fellowship"
Queen Creek, Az."

****

This is a story of hope and proof that no matter how ugly our beginnings, the human spirit is able to not only survive, but to overcome the past, move on and enjoy a full and happy life.

The author lays bare the dark secrets of his abusive childhood, giving us a shocking look at one of who-knows-how-many dysfunctional families that could be our neighbors—or ourselves.

Markie Crowley

CHAPTER 1

Growing Up In Kentucky

Writing any book is hard, but writing about one's own life is particularly difficult. On the one hand, you don't have to spend much time on research. I really didn't have to venture any farther then the storehouse of my own mind to write this book. Instead, I struggled mostly with what not to tell - as I know many things that could destroy people's lives, and hurting or destroying lives was not my intent. In fact, not wanting to do so is why it's taken me so many years to finally write this book.

At the same time, I feel the story should be told. What happened to my family resulted in so much hate and bitterness that it still threatens to overwhelm us fifty years later.

Just the last few years have I been able to talk about the things that took place in my early life. At age eleven I wasn't any different than other kids my age. We were a normal family at this time of my life. I was born the fourth child, but the first son of Gabriel and Norma Holbrook. Two more boys and two more girls would follow me.

Life was fun and exciting at this time. My Dad was a farmer and part time carpenter. When I was nine, Dad became the first independent coalminer to start his own coalmine, breaking away from the big controlling mining companies.

There was a good quality seam of coal running through our property, which was in the hill country of southeast Kentucky. At this time they took the coal out by vertical shaft mining, tunneling through the mountains, shearing or shafting up until the mountain was sitting on posts and beams, which became a very dangerous place to work.

In a few short years my Dad had become very successful. He kept working the farm and built a neighborhood grocery store. He sold his own produce, plus eggs, chicken, pork and fresh milk and butter. There weren't any laws against this in the forties. He also bought another hundred acre farm in the state of Virginia. It was about thirty five miles from the Kentucky farm. He built a small two bedroom house on this farm and rented it to a family to sharecrop. Most of it was sold through the Farmer's Market in the company owned mining communities that consisted of a hundred or more row houses. There were always eager buyers for fresh produce. The reason I'm going through this is to show the quality of businessman my father was.

My world changed one early spring morning. I was awakened with much activity as I could hear my dad groaning like he was in a lot of pain. My father died that morning from a heart attack. He was thirty eight years old. I remember the numbness and the unbelief that swept through my family. I remember my mother crying out to God asking Him how He could take her husband away leaving her with seven kids to raise. She had buried one daughter, Betty Jean, thirteen years earlier, who was only sixteen months old, and now, my dad. Mom would see a lot of grief in the next few years.

Almost sixty years have gone by, yet the fear in my mom's voice is still fresh in my memory. A week or so later, I picked up on my mom's fear when she sat me down at the kitchen table and explained that I had to take over as the man of the house, which also included taking over the running of the coal mines.

I had never had to worry about anything before, always being told what to do. Now I was expected to run a crew of men. I had spent a lot of time inside the mines with my dad and knew quite a bit about what was going on, but certainly not enough to take over as the boss.

The men had arrived and were standing outside talking with each other. They were probably wondering if they had a job at all. Jobs of any kind were hard to find and decent paying ones would have men lining up before daylight hoping to be hired.

I stuck my hands into my pockets to keep them from shaking off my arms and walked out to where the men were. With my head down and not making any eye contact, said with a shaky voice that my mom said it was ok for them to go to work. They eagerly grabbed their lunch pails, and said, "Thank you very much." I could sense they were as uncomfortable as I was. "Tell your mother we are very sorry about your father. He was the finest man I ever knew." I could only nod my head. I would let her know. I made a quick exit because the tears started to flow uncontrollably.

When I went back into the house, I heard my mother's mournful voice asking God why He had done this to her. I think that's when I started thinking God was punishing us. After breakfast, I started thinking about the things I had done that might be part of the trouble and I felt like God was singling me out for punishment, because to my horror, Mom said I had to go to the mines and make sure the men were working. I almost lost my breakfast. For some reason my twelve-year-old mind had not grasped the reality that I had to go inside the mines and oversee the employees. Once again the tears began to flow and once again my mom asked God why He was doing this to us.

I slipped my dad's rubber boots on because the mines had water a couple of inches deep in some places. The boots were about three sizes too big for me, making me realize that I wasn't ready to fill my father's shoes. Hard hats had not come on the scene as yet. My dad used a cloth hat that must have fit him pretty snug, because there was the carbide light that hung on the front of the hat. Like the shoes, the hat was too big for my twelve year-old head. Mom took a large safety pin and quickly reduced the hat two sizes. With this, off I went to be a miner. The mine was about three hundred yards from the house, and that was the longest and hardest three hundred yards I ever walked.

When I got inside the mines, I found the men very busy and after an hour or so one of the men came to me and said, "Son, I'm afraid you might get hurt in here, so why don't you go back outside? We are going to work just as hard as we did when your dad was here." This made good sense to me, so I quickly headed through the tunnel, and was glad when I stepped out into the fresh air.

After a couple of hours standing around, I became both bored and hungry, so when the men came out to have lunch, I headed home to have my lunch. I explained what the man said about me getting hurt, thinking I may not have to go back into the mines, but Mom said I had to stay there and count the number of tons of coal that was brought out. Mom sent my brother John back with me. This made the day go better. John was two years younger than me and we got along good, so we spent the afternoon throwing rocks at birds and anything else that got close enough to be hit by a rock. This shows the truth in the saying, "don't send a kid to do a man's job." The following morning found me once again entering the mines with my over-sized boots, my over-sized hat, and an under-sized desire to be there.

The day still had some good things in store. About ten A.M. Uncle Noah, my dad's brother, who lived about two miles from us, showed up. My heart jumped for joy when he informed me he was going to look after the mine for a while. "You need to get back in school," he said. Though I wasn't big on school, I whole-heartedly agreed with him.

"Yes, I'm getting way behind" I said. My Uncle Noah looked a lot like my dad, thick chest, large biceps and a hard worker. The over-sized boots didn't slow me down one bit. I headed for the outside and freedom so quick, that I forgot my lunch pail.

When I entered the house, I could see Mom was having a good day for the first time since Dad died. She had a sparkle in her eyes. She explained Uncle Noah was going to manage the mines and she was going to run the store and my brothers and sisters and I were going back to school, but I was expected to be home immediately after school to help with the chores.

We had horses and mules, two milk cows, three or four pigs and about two hundred chickens and they all had to be cared for twice a day. I had been helping with this since I was eight years old along with my brother and older sisters Evelyn and Wilma. I didn't like any kind of work, but this sure beat doing the coalmine thing. We all united as a family and got things done on the farm, not without some whining and complaining.

If things weren't bad enough, one-month later, my baby sister got pneumonia and after three days of high temperature, Mom took her to the Dr. He was with another patient, and my sister Rita died in my mother's arms. She was fifteen months old. This hurt us all deeply. The girls had become more like a mother to her and they were struggling greatly. There was more of "God, what have we done to deserve this?"

Warm weather brought on another problem. The fields had to be plowed again and gardens prepared and planted. Once again, as the oldest boy, I was expected to take the load of this, but I wasn't any different than any other twelve-year-old boy. My spirit rebelled.

It was also basketball season and I loved to play basketball. I became a complainer causing my mom a lot of hurt and anguish. I was supposed to start plowing the garden area early Saturday morning. Instead I sneaked off to the schoolyard and played basketball until noon. When I got home I found a very angry mother. She had already made her decision what the punishment was going to be, for a long switch was lying on the table. She immediately started using it on me. "I told you (whack) to start plowing. (Whack) If you are going to act like a little kid (whack) I will treat you like a kid." (Whack, Whack) So without lunch I headed to the barn and hitched up the mules for plowing. It was a long afternoon. I was mad and bitter, blaming my Dad for making me work, and especially blamed God for punishing me.

I was told later in life that my father was a good Christian man. My Mom said he prayed for hours before he died. I don't doubt this but I just don't remember any talks about Jesus shedding His blood for me. Maybe I just didn't understand, but I only remember going to church when someone died and we went to his or her funeral. The only Bible I was aware of was a huge Bible that had lots of pictures in it. These pictures always bothered me, like the one of Abraham standing over his son, Isaac with a huge knife, getting ready to take his life. They always showed people with anger and violence, fighting, killing, and throwing people to lions. When they showed pictures of Jesus, it was of Him walking around carrying a lamb in His arms, or pictures of Him being beaten or hanging on a cross. If the Bible isn't explained to children, it is easy to think that God wants to punish us, and if adults are asking God, "Why is all this bad stuff happening to us," kids quite easily pick up that our God is not a loving God.

After about three days of plowing the field my Dad's first cousin, Woodrow Holbrook, who lived on the farm next to us, stopped by. Woodrow was the son of my Dad's Uncle

Jess. He was about six years younger than my dad, and had just gotten out of the army.

Woody, as we called him, had never had a job to my knowledge, except the four years he spent in the service. He had started stopping by the store about every day, buying a soda pop and visiting with Mom. I think he was a year younger than Mom.

One day I was going by the store heading for the field with the mule, when Woody came out of the store and walked with me. He started talking and being very friendly, and me being the bashful type, I didn't have much to say back to him. Woody helped me hook the mules to the plow and to my surprise got behind the plow and started plowing. He made it look so easy. He was about one hundred eighty pounds and was very much in control of the mules and the plow. I, on the other hand was always battling with the plow. Soon the crooked rows I had made were starting to straighten out.

Woody was fun to be around. He was patient and didn't seem to get in a hurry, stopping to let the mules rest often. I found it real easy to like Woody. He spent most of the day helping me. Instead of a day of work, it turned into a day of pleasure. I was very proud of the work we had gotten done. We unhooked the mules and I took them back up to the barn and fed and watered them.

When I got back to the house, Mom had supper going and we were soon gathered around the table. I was extra hungry. Mom had fried pork, mashed potatoes, gravy and hot biscuits. All of us kids were healthy and were big eaters. In short order we consumed everything but the plates. Mom was in a good mood and bragged on how much garden I had gotten plowed and said the way I was putting away those biscuits and gravy we were going to need that extra garden. Everyone laughed. I sat up as tall as possible, thinking maybe I was a man, but deep inside I knew I was just a boy, and if Woody hadn't spent six hours helping me, I wouldn't be getting all that praise.

A couple weeks later, Uncle Noah came and helped me and the other kids plant the garden. He was still overseeing the mines. Woody was back in the store talking to Mom. He sure had taken a liking to soda pop, but I, along with Uncle Noah, thought it wasn't the soda that was bringing him by so often. I could tell he was upset about it. Later in the evening I heard him and Mom arguing. He never showed up next morning. I asked Mom if he was sick and she said no but he wouldn't be working at the mines any more. She gave me a bunch of reasons, but I could tell she was uncomfortable with the answer. A few weeks later I found out it was because of Woodrow.

The days were getting long and warm and my playtime had been limited to late evening and quite often into the night, so I was still tired and sleepy when Mom got me out of bed. I rebelled and said I wasn't going to go back to the mines and I was tired of hoeing corn and potatoes. I expected Mom to get her switch and give me a few "yes you will" swats, but instead she turned and walked into the kitchen.

My attitude changed when I saw her wipe tears from her eyes. So once again, I slipped on my over-sized shoes, got my hat and carbide lamp and started that long three hundred-yard walk to the mine. I felt bad for making Mom cry and felt sorry for her and myself. I missed playing with my friends. I sat outside of the mines and let the morning sunshine dry the tears.

I was almost asleep when I saw Woody coming up the hill toward the mine. He had his work clothes on and I almost started crying again when he told me Mom had hired him to be the working boss. His job title was called "mule skinner." It was because we used small mules to pull out the coal cars. The tears would be from happiness, not from sorrow.

Woodrow and his brother Floyd, Pug as we called him, was known for their drinking and fighting. Even though the county we lived in was a dry county, selling alcohol of any kind was illegal. There was a lot of moonshine available and when they had the money they would get a gallon of moonshine and stay drunk until it was gone. They would argue and cuss each other and quite often their father would be in the middle of it. He also had a weakness for moonshine.

For some reason the hill people of Kentucky like to yell, cuss and fight. Either they were downright mean or there was something in the moonshine that affected their brain.

Pug was two years younger than Woody and when drinking, was very dangerous. He had killed a man about five years earlier, had spent time in prison and was just now getting out. Woody got rid of the man that did the drilling and shooting the coal. Pug took his place. This was done after the day crew got through working. My brother John and I were paid twenty five cents a day to carry dynamite up to the mine. It took about three boxes a day. We soon learned how to drill and shoot coal. There weren't any rules in those days for kid's safety or anyone else's for that matter. We put the dynamite and blasting caps in the same sack, threw it up on our shoulder, not the least bit concerned. This knowledge of explosives helped me get a job with a logging Co. in Northern California some years later.

It amazes me to this day how adjustable one can be. It was only four months after losing our father and sister and already things were getting back to normal. Mom and Woody were openly seeing each other. They both seemed happy and laughed a lot with each other. Woody had gotten drunk three or four times since he had been working for Mom. He was what I called a happy drunk. There was silly joking and laughter, also being bolder about kissing Mom and grabbing her breasts. This bothered us kids, but didn't seem to bother Mom too much. She would laughingly slap his hand and say "shame on you. You stop that in front of the kids." I guess that meant it was all right when we weren't around.

My sister Evelyn was now seventeen years old and was dating a boy by the name of Billie. He started spending most of his time at our house, at least lunch and dinner. Bill was kind of timid and Evelyn argued with him a lot. She treated him more like one of us kids. She had quit school after dad died and had pretty much taken over the cooking and cleaning the house.

CHAPTER 2

Mom marries Woody

It was late summer when Mom and Woody came home from a day at the fair and carnival and informed us kids they had gotten married that afternoon. My sister Wilma who was fourteen years old started crying and said this drunken sot wasn't going to be her father. Mom halfheartedly scolded her. Woody said he wasn't trying to take the place of her father, "but I love your mother." I loved my Dad, but deep inside, my heart was thumping for joy. That meant I didn't have to be the man of the house anymore. Evelyn said her and Billie were going to get married. She was true to her word and next day they went to a justice of the peace and got married.

I could see Woody had been drinking quite a bit. He had straight sandy hair and he combed it back but the more he drank, the curlier it became. I later learned that when the curls hung down on his forehead, he became mean. Mom had been drinking some, and this was something new for her. They moved a bed out to the store into a large room where they kept sacks of cattle food and there was plenty of room for a bed. They spent two or three days out there before returning to the house. No more than a hundred feet separated the house from the store.

My brother John was stubborn and hot headed, even when he was a small child. He was now ten years old and had mixed emotions about Woody and the marriage. Shirley, eight and Charles, age four, was ok with it. I needed a man in my life and I liked Woody. Like I said about the ability to adjust, in a short time we were gathered around the table as a family. Now with Woody and Evelyn's husband, Bill, it took nine plates.

Bill and Evelyn were already having words with each other. Bill had moved into Evelyn's room, Wilma got booted out. She and Evelyn had shared a bed, so beds were at a premium. Our house only had three bedrooms. Woody and Mom took one. Evelyn and Bill took one. That left five kids to share the third bedroom. John, Chuck and I shared one bed; Shirley and Wilma shared the other. Wilma spent most of her nights on the couch in the living room. There was a stairway leading up to the attic. The area had been used for storage and canned goods. It had very low ceilings on the sides, but was six feet in the middle part. This was converted into a bedroom for Mom and Woody. Wilma and Evelyn seemed to fight a lot and as time went on, Wilma started spending a lot more time with a girlfriend who lived down the road a couple houses from us.

My life became more fun. Unlike my father, Woody wasn't very good in enforcing rules. Our work habits had gotten terrible. Us kids spent most of our time playing after school and wouldn't get home until dinnertime. Mom was getting pretty upset with us. She didn't like the job of disciplining us. In today's world it might be considered a normal family, but to me we had become very dysfunctional.

Evelyn, was now pregnant and doing most of the cooking. Wilma was gone a week or more at a time, but would help with the dishes when she was home. Wilma and Evelyn still argued with each other. John and I spent most all of our nonschool hours hunting and fishing or playing some kind of ball game. Shirley helped look after Chuck and with drying dishes. Woody was drinking more. He was spending more time in the grocery store with drinking buddies and less time looking after the mine. Mom was also pregnant and she too was falling into bad work habits. All of us kids, along with Mom and Woody, had spent many hours working the garden and fields of corn, now much of it was rotting on the vine.

When Dad was alive, getting the crops harvested was a big thing with him. The corn and hay was put up for the animals and a ton or more potatoes stored in the cellar and covered with straw, hundreds of jars of beans, tomatoes, green onions and other produce that could be dried, canned or stored through the winter. Without these commodities, one could have very easily starved during the cold winters and wet springs.

My Uncle Noah had not come around since Mom and Woody got married. Then one evening I was on my way home from the school yard, where I spent much of my time playing basketball, when Uncle Noah who owned a coal truck stopped and asked me if I wanted a ride home. Though it was only half a mile home, I eagerly jumped in the cab with him. The road was so rough and bumpy, I could have walked faster, but I was glad to spend time with my Uncle Noah.

After asking me how I was doing, he asked many questions about Mom and Woodrow. I could tell he wasn't very impressed with the way things were heading. He asked if Woody was mean to us kids. I told him that he was real good to us. Then he asked how come the fields hadn't been harvested. I could feel my face getting red because I knew I was part of the problem. "I don't know," I answered.

"Well, don't you think it's about time you were finding out?" Noah asked sharply. His tone let me know he was expecting more from me.

"I think we are going to start tomorrow," I lied.

"Should have started two weeks ago," he said with the sharpness still in his voice. "Word is going around that your Dad's mine is losing money. I'm told over at the ramp the production is way down, and they are docking every load that comes in for too much slate."

The company that bought our coal owned the ramp. Each truckload of coal was weighed, then backed up a ramp and the coal was dumped into railroad cars. There was a four inch seam of slate that ran through the middle of the coal seam. The slate was three times heavier than coal; it was white textured and wouldn't burn. When mixed too heavy with the coal, it would plug up the grates in stoves. A small amount was expected because when the coal was shot with dynamite some would be blown into small pieces, but all that could be removed, was expected to be taken out at the mines.

I was more than glad when the coal truck stopped at our house. I felt like I had just gotten a whipping. Uncle Noah must have read my face as he quickly said, "son, I'm not blaming you, but Woodrow and Pug neither one would ever work any longer than it took to buy a gallon of moonshine."

I was shedding tears by now. When I started to open the door, he stuck a dime in my hand. I hesitated to take it, but he said, "Oh, come on and take it." I took it and hurriedly jumped out and into the house. Under different conditions I would have been glad to accept a dime. That would buy a soda pop and a candy bar. I kept hearing Uncle Noah's words and my mind became troubled as I started remembering the many hard days work Dad had put into getting the mine and farm producing good.

The next morning was Saturday and after breakfast I asked Mom if she was going to start canning. She said she had to get the jars washed and ready but would probably start the next week.

"Well, Uncle Noah said we are going to lose our crops if we didn't get it in soon." She gave me a real dirty look and informed me she wasn't married to Noah and he had better mind his own business and keep his nose out of her business. I made mistake number two when I told her Uncle Noah had said the mine was going broke. (Not his exact words.) I thought Mom was going to slap me. "What have you been telling Noah?" Mom asked.

"Nothing" I answered. "He just told me that was the talk over at the Ermine ramp." Now Woodrow gave Mom a mean look and got up from the table, shoving back the dishes.

Mom questioned me about all Noah had said. I told her about docking every load for slate. She seemed disturbed about everything. Wilma showed up about that time and Mom took her frustrations out on her for not being home and helping with chores. By now, I regretted ever opening my mouth.

In short order, John, Wilma, and I were sent to the garden with orders to start digging the potatoes. Evelyn's husband, Bill, was sent to oversee us. He had a real dislike for work and usually managed to avoid it. He was one of the reasons the mine wasn't doing good. He hated loading coal and wasn't doing much of it, but still getting paid the same as the ones that was working hard. This was causing hard feelings among the other men. Bill had been raised in town and didn't have any knowledge of mine work or gardening. He had been talking about taking Evelyn to Detroit, Michigan and going to work in the auto factory.

For the next week or two we were sent to the garden and we worked until dark. Everybody got involved. Woody had a nephew, Jimmie Hall, one of his sisters' sons. Jim was two years older than me. His father had gotten drowned about four years earlier. Woody was paying Jim twenty five cents per hour to help harvest the corn. We got relief from the labor when a heavy rain stopped everything. It never got started again.

A couple days after the rain, the evening was cool and we were all in the house, except Woody. He hadn't gotten back from the Ermine Coal Co. where he went to pick up our weekly check. Then we heard one of the "Yahoos" yells. That meant that Woody was home and he was drunk. One of his buddies was with him. Woodys' hair was hanging in curls on his forehead. This meant he was very drunk. His friend was staggering all over the place.

All of us kids became nervous, as they were loud. Mom was mopping the kitchen floor and me and the other kids were all gathered in the dining room so we could be close to her. We could see she was nervous, too. Woody came into the kitchen and without a word, punched Mom in the face with his fist, breaking her nose, and glasses, cutting her under the eyes. Mom went down letting out a frightening scream. Woody took a step forward and had raised his foot to kick her, when he slipped on the wet floor and fell backwards. This gave Mom a few needed seconds to get her senses together. Though she was now heavy with child, she ran out the back door. Within seconds all of us kids followed her like a swarm of bees.

The barn was about one hundred yards from the house. Mom ran behind the barn and was gasping for breath when we caught up with her. "Oh children, I'm hurt bad" she said between sobs. I don't think I have ever been more scared. Mom was a free bleeder and the blood was still pouring from her nose. Fear turned to hate and anger. I wanted to get a gun and kill him, but Mom and the girls said, "No, they will kill you."

Just at that time we heard Woody yell, "Norma, you get yourself in here right now."

"Oh God, we can't let him find us," she said. I quickly lost my nerve and followed Mom as she dashed for the woods. We continued hiking for about half a mile before Mom felt safe enough to stop for any length of time. With all the hiking we were doing, Mom's nose was still bleeding. She had torn a piece of her dress and managed to use pieces to plug her nose. This helped stop the blood flow along with the long rest. As we huddled together trying to decide what we were going to do, only then did it dawn on me that Evelyn's husband Billy was with us. I was both glad and mad, because on one hand it made us feel safe and on the other, mad because he was twenty years old and should have stood up to Woodrow.

The nights were getting cold and the previous rain had left the ground and brush wet under the trees. Mom had been a light smoker. I don't know how long, but she would never smoke in front of Dad. But since she had been with Woody she smoked openly and so did most of us kids. Mom was wearing an apron with pockets. She had both cigarettes and matches. Even though we were all shivering from the cold damp night, she was afraid to light a fire for fear Woody would see the flames or smell the smoke. So we huddled together and talked in whispers. Sleep would come and go.

Our house sat in a small valley and was surrounded by steep hills. Once one got on top of the hill, you could walk the ridges. It was easy going and that's where we were now.

I was very familiar with the mountains. I had hunted in them since I was six or seven years old and knew them at night within a three or four mile radius. I didn't think Woody was in any shape to climb to where we were even if he knew where we were. We owned a hunting dog named Bingo. Dad had bought him for me when I was about four. We grew up together and Bingo was very protective of me and the other kids. He seemed to know there was something wrong. He probably picked up on our fear. We all became awake when Bingo started growling and looking down the hill. Everyone bolted like a spooked herd of deer. I was the one that knew the mountain best so I took the lead. We hiked another half a mile, crossing onto our neighbors' property and down into the valley where we spent the night. There was a small creek that ran through it. We were in need of water and Mom was able to wash and clean the blood from her face. She looked terrible. Her nose was swollen and the right eye was black and swollen shut. When it was dark it didn't look so bad, but now that it was daylight, you could see her swollen face. Shirley would look at Mom and cry, but the older kids and I were building up hate and resentment toward Woody.

I can't remember ever being so glad to see the sun peak over the mountain. We were all chilled to the bone. None of us were dressed any more than a light shirt. Mom had wrapped her apron around Chuck, who had only a T-shirt and short pants on. He was also bare foot. It was a normal thing to go without shoes in the summer. But this was late fall and there were lots of briars and thistles that couldn't be seen at night.

Wilma, and Bill, and I took turns carrying Chuck. Though we were tired, scared and hungry, in the warmth of the morning, we curled up in a little grassy meadow and slept like we were in a luxury hotel.

If I was the one reading this book, I would be asking the question why we didn't go to the police or to a neighbor for help. The only way to get there was to walk. No one in our family could drive. That included Woodrow. Dad had left a beautiful 1936 Buick, but it hadn't been started in months. If we had gone to the police, they would have waited until the next day, and by then the whiskey would be all gone and everything would be back to normal. Like the neighbors, no one wanted to get involved with a drunken mountain man; one could get killed, which happened too often.

It was a common thing for a woman to get beaten up by her husband in the hill country. There were lots of abusive husbands. The women usually stayed out of the way for a day or two and then went back to their regular routine of cooking and cleaning, milking cows and washing baby diapers. That is exactly what happened to us.

By noon we were hungry and knew we had to make some kind of decision. So we started back over the hill to our property. When we got close enough to see the house, Mom said someone had to sneak down close enough to see if Woody was still there. Mom felt Bill would be the logical one to go, but he had a hundred reasons why he shouldn't be the one.

Evelyn was giving Bill a dirty look so Mom turned to me and with pleading in her one good eye, she asked me to go check things out. The swelling had pretty much gone down from Mom's face. Her right eye was visible but very blood shot.

John went with me and we quietly sneaked up to where we could see the front of the house. We saw Woody sitting on the cement steps. He was holding his head and gagging like he was real sick. Boldness came over me. To be honest, it was probably more from hunger than from having nerve.

I walked up within fifteen feet of him, leaving room to run. I shuffled my feet to get his attention. He looked up kind of surprised, and asked "where have you been, son, and where is your mom?" He had never called me son before and this made me feel everything was going to be ok. "Are you sick?" I asked.

"I'm sick as a dog. Go see if you can find your mom and see if she will come and fix me something to eat. My belly is on fire from that moonshine."

I wandered slowly around the house until I was out of his sight and then ran quickly back to where Mom and the kids were and told her what Woody had said. She thought for a minute then said "Kids, let's go home." We all went through the back door that led into the kitchen. The mop bucket was still sitting in the place where it had been left the night before. Wilma grabbed the mop bucket and the mop and I got busy getting a fire started in the cook stove. Soon the smell of food was filling the air. It was early evening and everyone was ready for dinner.

Looking back I can see where that was the place we should have taken a stand, but at the time we were just happy to be home where there was food and warm clothes. When Woody saw Mom, he acted surprised and asked her "what happened to you?"

Tears came into Moms eyes as she answered, "You know what happened."

Woody replied "I swear to God I don't remember anything since I drank that rot gut whiskey yesterday. Why, you know I wouldn't hurt you."

Even then I wondered why he didn't ask any more questions about it. Instead he started talking about getting robbed after he had cashed the check. He had stopped at the road-house to have a few beers. There was a man there that he had never seen before and the man told Woody that he had bought five gallon of good moonshine at a real good price and he would let Woody have a gallon at the same price if he wanted it. They went out to where he had the moonshine in the man's car. Woody said they had a few drinks and the man came home with him. He didn't remember any more until the next morning when he woke up and the man and his money were gone.

Whether Mom bought the story or not, I don't know, but she became very worried about being able to pay the men. Little did I know that this was going to become a way of life for us; even as hard as jobs were to find, it was getting harder to keep good men.

The beatings became more frequent and we spent more and more time running and hiding out in the woods. In the winter when it was freezing or below, we would hide back in the coalmine. Though it was dark and damp, (it was about forty five to fifty degrees) not warm, but much better than the freezing rain or snow. Those times outside were almost unbearable, especially if there was a wind. Sometimes we would hide in people's barns. We would crawl inside the loose hay and find rest and warmth and be able to steal a few hours of sleep.

This was getting harder and harder to do as Mom had given birth to Jack. Our new brother was only two months old when he spent his first night outdoors. John and I got to be very professional at sneaking into our neighbor's houses and stealing canned food. No one locked their fruit house or cellar, as we called it. The most important thing was getting acquainted with the dogs so they wouldn't bark too much. We also made a point to get familiar with the order they had the canned fruit and vegetables in. We would check this out when we were playing with our neighbor kids. I always felt bad when we took their food. They had worked hard in getting the stuff stored, and they were quite often in worse shape financially than we were, but when there is a bunch of hungry little kids, you do whatever you have to do to survive.

Just before Woody beat Mom up the first time, we were trying to get our crops put away, but the biggest share was left in the field to rot and go to waste. Evelyn's husband Bill wanted Evelyn to get out of the hill country and go with him to Detroit, but she said she wasn't going to leave her brothers and sisters. She felt she was needed to help so after the second trip out in the cold, sleeping on the damp ground, he showed that he was much wiser than we were. He packed his suitcase and walked away, never to be heard from again. By now Evelyn's daughter, Phyllis was born and she and her dad would never see each other. No one seemed to miss Bill and he was soon forgotten.

Phyllis and Jack were only one month difference in age and it became real difficult some times to keep Jack and Phyllis from crying while we were hiding out, especially when we were hiding in someone's barn and they would come to milk or feed their animals. We tried to sneak out before daylight, but sometimes the farmer would start doing his chores before daylight. We would hide in an empty barn stall or in the loft where the hay was kept. Mom and Evelyn got faster getting their breast out and in the baby's mouth than Billie the Kid drawing his six- shooter.

Like I said before, it never ceases to amaze me of how adjustable we humans are. Even though this abuse and fear was always present, sandwiched in between all the bad, there are good memories of days spent hunting and days camping in the mountains. Woody was a good camper. Woody, Mom, John, Baby Jack and I would hike four or five hours into the mountains that divided Kentucky and Virginia. We would carry our groceries in grain sacks and spend three or four days hunting and picking wild huckleberries. Sometimes we would kill a pheasant or squirrel. That would highlight our dinner. Mom and Woody would act like newlyweds. There was always hot coffee simmering in the hot coals and they would talk late into the night until the wood on the open fire would burn down and the shadows and darkness of the night would close in around us and we would drift off into a sound, peaceful sleep.

I would awaken to the roar of a new fire popping and snapping sending sparks high into the air. The heat was welcome as the mornings were cool and moist from the dew. We didn't own sleeping bags, and only carried light blankets. I would watch the streak of sunlight as it pushed back the early morning shadows. Its brilliance was soon turning the autumn hardwoods. It's hard to describe its beauty as the sunrays danced off the yellow, brown and golden leaves. Autumn is so beautiful in the hill country of Kentucky. The beechnut, hickory, larch, maple and oak trees, were all showing off their individual colors. But too soon it was back to the drinking.

The coalmine with our main income closed down. I went with Woody to pick up the last check. We had a man that was renting a small house from us, who also knew how to drive. Dad had bought a dump truck just a month before he died. Mom's brother drove it until the mine closed down. Now the truck was parked because neither Mom nor Woody knew how to drive. The renter's name was K.R Webb. So Woody got him to drive us to Ermine to pick up our last check. Mom had me go along; I'm sure hoping Woody wouldn't get drunk. That was the first time I can remember eating in a restaurant. I had a chili -dog and orange pop. I still like chili- dogs, but none ever tasted as good as that first experience. On the way home Woody couldn't get past that flickering light of the Coalminer's Inn. You are probably way ahead of me if you are thinking Woody started hitting the bottle. You are right. We went in and sat at the counter. Woody bought me a soda and potato chips. A woman came out of a door that looked like it went into the kitchen. She was a very attractive lady, wearing a big smile and too much rouge. She came over and whispered something to Woody and he shook his head "yes." Then she whispered in his ear again and they both looked at me and laughed. At the same time, she winked at me with very flirty eyes. My face turned so red it must have lit up the whole room. Woody turned to me and said he and K.R were going to the back and have a beer and would be back in a few minutes. I wanted to ask him to not start drinking, but the cute brunette with the sparkly brown eyes gave me that wink and my face lit up the room again and I became brain dead for the next few minutes.

After half an hour had gone by, I started getting nervous and was very uncomfortable with the steady stream of truckers as well as businessmen coming and going through the back door. A different woman would show up every few minutes and return back through the door quite often with a man following her. I was so naive. I didn't know this was a house of prostitution, let alone that I was sitting in one. About an hour and a half later, Woody and K.R. came out. Woody's hair was getting that curly look. They were both laughing and they both were carrying something in a paper bag, which turned out to be moonshine.

E.R. seemed to be in better shape than Woody or he held his whiskey better. I was scared to start the drive home. Not only was I concerned about his driving, but also I was worried about what Mom was going to say to me when we got home. They had each bought a pint and that is enough moonshine to make four people drunk. I was sure hoping their good mood would last. They were kidding each other and laughing about what the girls said or did. K.R. said the next time they stopped he was going to take me into the back room. I blushed and said he wasn't going to get me in there, but I secretly wanted to see what went on back there. I was now 13 and my hormones were getting very active.

I was glad to see our house come into view. Woodsy' hair was now curly and another troubling sign was that he was gritting his teeth. This was always a sign he was going to be mean. I hurriedly went into the house, warning Mom. I saw fear come on her face and she gave quick orders to the other kids to grab clothes and food and hide it outside in case we had to make a run for it. But Woody came in and sat down on the couch and started playing with his son, Jack and in a little while, he fell asleep. Everyone let out a sigh of relief. John and I went to the barn to feed the chickens and hogs.

I was chopping wood for the morning fire and John had his arms loaded with wood, when we saw Mom and the kids running toward us heading for the barn. Mom was carrying Jack and the other kids had grabbed blankets and food. As they got closer, I could see Mom's dress was half torn off, but she looked unhurt. Shirley was carrying baby Phyllis and Evelyn was carrying Chuck. I became instantly angry and started toward the house with the double bladed axe. I told Mom "I have been run out of my house for the last time. I'm going to kill that lousy drunk." I started crying and saying over and over, "I'm going to kill him." Mom's fear became maximized as she and Evelyn grabbed me and started taking the axe out of my hands. I was getting to be a good- sized boy and was fairly stout.

It looked like I was going to win the tussle when Mom cried out saying, "Oh God, what are you trying to do to me now? How much more can I take?" My love for my Mom overpowered my killing instinct, so I let loose of the axe. Evelyn grabbed it, and threw it over in the tall weeds. John was still holding the armload of wood. Mom said, "Hurry son, let's get out of here before it's too late."

John said he wasn't going to go and Mom got all worked up again and she started crying and calling out to God. Chuck and Jack were nervous wrecks as was Shirley. They started crying.

We were all standing in a circle as though we were having a crying contest, when we saw Woody coming toward the barn. He yelled, "Every one of you get back here." We all started running but John. He just stood there holding his armload of wood. "Get back here or I'm going to burn the dad -burn house down!" Woody yelled. Mom grabbed John by the back of his shirt, jerking him and the wood about a foot in the air. So once again we became like frightened animals and headed for the forest.

By now we had done this so much, we had a routine that we went through, even to having favorite little places to sleep. It may be a sink- hole in the ground where the autumn leaves piled up, or making a soft bed where we had stacked cedar bows. We spent most of the night talking about what was going to happen to us. Mom was in a weepy mood and spent most of the night crying. She said that she would get a divorce but Woody would still live next door and would always be trouble when he got drunk.

Somehow we came to the conclusion that we had to kill him, but in a way that it didn't look like murder. If we burned the house down with him in it, it would work, except we would be homeless. The little three- room house that K.R.

was renting was too small for us, because without Woody, there were still eight of us. We finally decided that poison was the only answer, but the only kind of poison we had any knowledge of was D-Con, a rat poison. It was new on the market and it really worked well, but how were we going to arrange for him to eat it? It was finally decided that I would slip in the house, put the poison into the pot of beans that was setting on the stove. We sold rat poison in the store and I knew where we had a key hidden. I was to get two boxes, take all but one or two bowls of beans out of the pot then dump the two boxes of D-Con into the remaining beans. We would wait a day and make sure he had eaten the beans before going home. Well, killing him with the axe while I was mad didn't bother me a great deal, but to deliberately murder someone started making me real nervous, especially being as how I got picked to be the hit man.

Now I started talking like my Mom. "Lord what have I done, that you have brought all this on me?" I had one more suggestion for Mom. Maybe we could move into the place in Virginia and let Woody have this one.

"Well how in the world are we going to make it, living off that farm?" Mom asked. "Besides, that house is way too small for all of us." I had to admit she had me there. We just hadn't seemed to grab hold of Dad's ambition, but compared to what we were doing it seemed like a fair exchange. After three or more times of 'what if' Mom must have decided that it wasn't too good of an idea, but I will have to admit there did come times when I wished I had gone through with the D-Con idea.

But like I said, we had worked out a routine and the next afternoon found us wandering back home. We picked up the scattered kindling wood and soon the beans on the stove were heating up. Woody, as usual said he didn't remember anything, but as we all sat around the table, and with every bite of beans, I knew we all were remembering what we had planned earlier for those beans.

Mom was now three or four months pregnant with Woody's second child. He wasn't drinking as much now that the money supply had run out. The grocery store wasn't making any money. When Dad was alive he would make a weekly trip to the wholesale outlet for supplies. He also took advantage of the crops he raised and sold, plus the beef, pork, chickens, eggs, and milk. But now, Mom had a supply truck to deliver things to the store sometimes, but it was a 14mile round trip and she ordered such small quantities that the profits from the store were much smaller.

Woody had always been kind of jealous of Mom when men would come into the store and stay a little longer than he felt they should. He would question Mom and sometimes accuse Mom of flirting with them. One day Woody, who had been drinking, but not yet drunk, was sitting on the front porch, when a single man who had been interested in Mom before she married Woody, stopped by the store. I could see he didn't like it, and after about five minutes, when the man still hadn't come out, Woody got up and headed for the store. It was real common for people passing by, whether walking or driving, to stop in for a soda and spend a few minutes visiting and swapping news. I was worried Woody would start slapping Mom around after the man left, but instead the man went flying through the door with Woody right behind him. The man jumped up and started toward his car and Woody started kicking him in the rear end. Woody told him to get his rear end off his property and to never stop there again. The man must have gotten the message, because he never stopped there anymore.

The store closed permanently after that. When we ran out of something it was never replaced. I think there is a saying in the book of Proverbs that a fool eats his seeds instead of planting a crop. It began to look like that verse could be applied to us because things went down hill from then on.

A new problem was in the making. Woody now had his eyes on the girls and it wasn't long before it was his hands that were doing the grabbing. When one of the girls would walk by, he would grab a breast or stick his hand up their dress. Now one would have thought this would have been the last straw and Mom would have kicked him out, but instead she turned on the girls with a deep jealousy. Then she did something that was supposed to solve the problem. She and Woody moved into the store by adding a cook stove, table, a couch and a couple wooden chairs. Jack their son lived with them, but all of us other kids weren't allowed to come inside their home and it stayed that way until our brother Jerry was born. Then Mom and Woody moved back in the house with us. All of her kids were born at home, and when Jerry was born the Dr. told Mom that if she had any more kids, it could kill her. He said she had been close to losing the baby and her life, too.

The girls took good care of Mom and the baby for a couple weeks while she got some needed rest. The sexual problem had escalated since they were back with us. Woody was getting bolder and more aggressive as time went on. He was now coming into their bedroom at night and would crawl into bed with them. When they would scream and jump out of bed, he would laugh like it was supposed to be funny.

Wilma and Shirley started staying with girl friends when Woody was drinking. Mom and Woodrow decided to trade houses with K.R. Webb. He moved into the storehouse and Mom and Woody moved into the house on the hill, as we called it. It sat about one hundred yards from the home we were living in. This put a little more distance between Woody and the girls. Like before, we weren't allowed to go inside their home. It had gotten to the place where this wasn't a problem except the food supply was getting lower all the time. We weren't doing any better at farming. We still had a few eggs, but we weren't selling them anymore. Like the groceries in the store, we weren't restocking and up the road would, run out. I think we all knew this would happen, but no one did anything about it.

John and I spent most of our time fishing or hunting. We had a twenty-two rifle and both of us were good shots. The rabbits and squirrels didn't have much of a chance if we got a shot at them. Mom and Woody didn't seem to care if we went to school or not and we got further and further behind. We had a teacher that seemed concerned, and it was no secret what kind of life style we were living. Kids tell other kids and they tell parents, but no one ever came by to check. The teachers must have thought they were helping us when they passed us into the next grade, though our grades were mostly C's, D's or F's. I guess we were expected to go into the coal-mines. That's what most of the young men did. There were more independent coalmines in the area since Dad led the way.

We were down to our last three laying hens, and it was a race to see who would get the eggs. Our meals were now mostly biscuits and gravy, so an egg was a treat. We were down to one cow and soon she would stop milking. Mom and Woody got twenty dollars a month in rent from K.R. From that we got a fifty pound bag of flour, a can of baking powder, a package of coffee, a sack of cornmeal and enough brown beans to last about two weeks. A box of twenty-two shells cost twenty cents. The stores redeemed pop bottles for one cent each and I scrounged the neighborhood for them. There were fifty-two shells to a box, so with this, John and I added an occasional rabbit or squirrel to our menu.

It was a sad day when K. R. moved out. Woody had been making a lot of sexual advances to his wife while he was working. One evening Woody had been drinking and had stopped by KR.'s place. His wife wouldn't let Woody in so he started kicking the door. She grabbed a loaded shotgun and fired through the door. It was a fairly heavy door and that probably saved him from being a cripple for life. His legs and thighs still took a lot of number six birdshot along with wood slivers. The doctor said if it had been buckshot or had been two feet higher, it could have killed him. K.R. loaded up his wife and a few personal belongings and we never heard from him again.

We were never able to understand why Mom continued to stay with Woody. She now was making excuses for him. One night we were awakened by gunshots and we could hear the bullets hitting the side of the house where our bedrooms were. Woody had an automatic pistol and as fast as it was firing, we felt that's what he was shooting. We all moved to the opposite side of the house and spent most of the night huddled together. It was a long, fearful night. We were scared for Mom and the boys and we felt he may have killed all of them. We decided if we didn't hear from Mom soon after daylight, we were going to try and get help from someone. Shortly after daylight, we heard someone chopping wood and we all breathed a sigh of relief when we heard Mom talking to the boys. She was talking louder than normal and we knew she was letting us know she was all right.

John and I walked up to our Uncle Noah's to see if he could or would help us. He wasn't very happy with Mom and he said she was going to let that family destroy her and us kids and he didn't seem too happy with us kids either. If he only knew we weren't very pleased with ourselves, either. He took advantage of our presence and let us help him with some road work. He had been gathering rocks to fill in the holes and ruts in the road where the bottom of his truck had been dragging. He had about one half of a mile of private road and to my eyes it all needed filled in. As I looked around the farm, I saw at least one hundred piles of rock and the biggest wheelbarrow I had ever seen. I figured I would be lucky to push the wheelbarrow empty let alone loaded with seventy five to one hundred pounds of rock. I was glad when Uncle Noah said for John and I to load it and he would do the wheeling. After a couple hours, even as muscular as Uncle Noah was, he had enough of that monstrosity.

We got in Uncle Noah's truck and started back down the road to our house at a snail's pace. I could have walked faster but it was fun to ride in a truck. When we got home, the girls said Mom had come by to let them know she was all right. Uncle Noah must not have felt too safe because when he reached up by the window to check out the bullet holes, I could see he was carrying a pistol in his waistband. Two bullet holes weren't more than a foot from the window and if it had come through the window, it could easily have killed one of us.

I could see Uncle Noah was disturbed. He said that he was going into town and talk to the sheriff. We had mixed feelings about that. We were both glad and scared. We had grown up to be leery of the law enforcement. No one in the hill country trusted them. I suspect it was because so many people in that area were moon shiners. That meant they made and sold illegal whiskey. I had come upon stills while hunting and I would get out of there as quick as possible. Most of them had guns and they were well known for using them. It was an unspoken rule in the hill country that one doesn't squeal on his neighbors, even if you didn't like them.

Late that evening, a deputy sheriff stopped at out house and asked a lot of questions. "Did you see who was doing the shooting?"

We said, "No, but we're sure those bullet holes are from last night."

He said, "The only way to tell for sure is to tear out the wall and try and find the bullets, if that's what these holes are from."

Evelyn asked if he would fix the wall back and he said "No" we would have to have it fixed.

She said "Then, don't tear it out." The deputy said he would go up and talk to Woody and Mom. We never heard another word from him or Uncle Noah any more.

Maybe this would be a good time to acquaint the reader with some of the things that went on in the county we lived in. A lot of the law enforcement was involved in bootlegging. They had runners that would buy direct from the moon shiners, fifty to one hundred gallons at a time and some was delivered to the houses that were owned or approved of by the law enforcement, which meant a big kickback or they wouldn't be in business long. It wasn't any different than the Mafia in the larger cities. There was also a daily run of illegal whiskey going to Michigan, Chicago and New York.

They owned the Roadside Inn that Woody visited often. It was one of the more popular ones in the area that you could buy beer, whiskey, and gamble and of course your favorite woman for a price. So you see this Mafia controlled the whole county. The deputy that went to see Woody may have been his drinking buddy. We never felt safe in that bedroom after that so we moved the bed to the opposite wall and out of line of the window.

Now with K.R. gone, there wasn't anyone around to drive the dump truck or perhaps it was pride that stopped Mom and Woody from asking anybody. It was a scary time when Woody talked Mom into driving the truck. About all she knew was that the key turned the switch on, and push a button to start the engine. She didn't know the clutch from the brake, or one gear from the other. It had a Ford engine that started real easy and a five- speed transmission with a two - speed rear end. But if it had only one gear, it wouldn't have made any difference, because to my knowledge, she never took it out of second gear. First gear was five miles per hour wide open, second gear was fifteen, maybe, but I have never seen her drive more than ten miles per hour. After a couple hours, Mom learned that the clutch had to be held in to get the truck started. A week later she was still trying to coordinate letting the clutch out without killing the engine. She often forgot to put the clutch back in when she wanted the truck to stop. This caused the truck to jump and buck and unnerve Mom until she would have jumped out and let it go had not Woody reminded her to put the clutch in. Reverse was never mastered and more often than not a ditch, bank or a tree, and at least once the barn stopped her.

She would have given up but Woody would just laugh and have fun. If she ran into the ditch he would get the mule and pull the truck out. After a couple months of practice on the farm, Mom got up enough nerve to venture out on the old country road where we lived. The road was narrow and bumpy and just wide enough for vehicles to pass if they were reasonably good drivers. That's not the category Mom was in. If I had to pick a category, it would have to be like my grades in school, extra bad, although Mom drove for the next couple of years. Her driving skills never improved. She was always uptight and nervous and so were all the neighbors. When they saw Mom and the old dump truck coming, they would start screaming for kids to get inside the house, and then run around scooping the chickens and live stock as far away from the road as possible. Then shaking their head in bewilderment, as Mom and Woody would go chugging by at five to ten miles per hour. One thing I can say about Mom, she would always give everyone a chance to get out of her way. When she went around a corner she would honk the horn all the way around. There were lots of curves and lots of honking.

I remember one trip I may still be shaking a little from. My grandfather lived in Virginia, only five miles from our Virginia farm. One day Mom and Woody decided to take a ton of coal to him. Woody's Dad had a bunch of young pigs six or eight weeks old and Woody decided to take two pigs and trade for moonshine. He got a grain sack, and cut holes in the sack just large enough for the pigs' head to stick through. They went in the cab with Mom, Woody, John, Jack and, Jerry. I rode in the back of the truck with the coal. I guess the pigs outranked me, but even with the coal dust blowing in my face, the air was much better than in the truck cab. Things went pretty good, although the bumpy road made it very uncomfortable. The lumps of coal were about the size of a two pound coffee can and they were shifting and rolling around under me. It was easier to stand up and hold on the sideboard. It was like going down a wild river in a flat bottom boat. But the constant horn honking was both irritating and embarrassing. Mom was getting ready to take on a new challenge, driving on a blacktop road with two lanes. With the old truck revved up in second gear we headed east to Virginia. Now on the dirt road where Mom learned to drive, when she would meet another vehicle, she would pull over and stop until the vehicle passed. On the dirt road this wasn't a big deal, but Mom continued this practice out on the highway. There weren't very many cars on the road, but the ones that were behind us chose to stay that way, because Mom drove in the middle of the road and only got over when she saw an oncoming car. Of course she would stop until the car passed and she never discovered how to look in the mirror for traffic behind her. Now days that would have led to "road rage." But when Mom would stop without any kind of signal and her constant honking because of the curvy mountainous roads, it so unnerved the people following us that they stayed a good distance back. I had a bird's eye view of their frustration and it's just as well Mom didn't know what was going on behind her.

I was more than glad when Mom pulled over to a wide spot where there was a water trough. The water was drinkable and could also be used for over-heated radiators. There were a couple picnic tables and a well used trail that led to an outhouse off in the distance. As soon as the truck stopped, Mom headed off in that direction, but with the smells coming from the cab of the truck, I think it might have been too late. It was a powerful odor flowing up and I don't think it was just the pigs.

I didn't smell too good either. Those people we were holding up for the past hour were stopping. Woody and John were getting water to wash the truck out so I took this opportunity to stroll off into the distance. Things were peaceful when I got back to the truck. Woody was visiting with some people that he had gone to school with. They were laughing and asking each other "do you remember the time that?" "HO! HO! HO!" went the other. John looked real pale and said he had gotten sick from the smell and I could ride in the cab for a while. I said no way was I getting in with those smelly pigs. We argued back and forth for a while, so Mom said we both could ride back there. Woody could hold Jerry, and Jack, who was over two years old, could sit by himself.

The pigs were squealing and shoving each other around whether they were fighting or playing I couldn't tell. Maybe they were blaming each other for being in the sack.

In short order we were loaded up and chug chugging down the road again. Time passed quicker with John to visit with, but we both became very alert when we saw a train approaching. The tracks crossed the road we were traveling on and we got very scared when we realized Mom didn't see it. We were coming into a little town and her mind was focused straight ahead. At ten miles per hour we could have jumped out, but of course we didn't want any of our family hurt. So we started screaming "a train is coming" but they couldn't hear us so the truck kept chugging up the road. John got a block of coal and threw it down on the cab of the truck. That got their attention. Mom turned to roll down the window and saw that the train and us were going to reach the crossing at the same time. She slammed on the brakes, forgetting to push the clutch in and kids and pigs went everywhere. John and I just about got thrown from the truck. After the train went by, Woody yelled up and asked if we were all right. We told him we were, although the sharp edges on the blocks of coal separated us from a lot of our skin. It sounded like Mom was a total wreck even if the truck wasn't. She was crying out, "Oh Blessed Lord; I could have killed us all. Lord if you get us home safe, I'll never drive again."

The carburetor had gotten flooded and the truck wouldn't start, so we were stranded in the middle of the road. Of course, this gave Mom a chance to calm down a little bit. The truck finally fired up again, but big problems were in the making. When we came to a quick stop, either the pigs or the kids had engaged the lever that raises the dump bed. It took a few seconds before I knew the bed was rising up. By now the truck was getting ready to cross the railroad track. With both John and I yelling, the bed continued to rise. John and I were holding onto the sideboards, but finally had to let go, and we shot to the back of the truck bed with the coal. The tailgate didn't open, but about half the coal went over the tailgate and onto the railroad track. Mom didn't know anything was wrong until a couple of young men ran alongside the truck and flagged her down. Mom didn't know how to disengage the lever to lower the bed, so the man showed her what to do. They also said they would clean the coal off the railroad track if Mom would give them the coal. "Oh yes, you are welcome to every piece of it." Mom said.

This was the longest two hours of my life. Mom said, "I'm going to turn this truck around and get back home while we are still all in one piece."

Woody finally got her calmed down. "It's only five more miles up to the picnic area. We can stop there and have lunch and let the kids play for awhile," he said.

This would be our half way mark, the Kentucky- Virginia state line. Mom had made up some bologna sandwiches and potato salad. Mom was still a nervous wreck, but cranked the old truck up one more time and set our sites on Virginia. As bad as it was, it could have been worse. If she had gone another twenty feet, we would have taken out a power line and possibly gotten electrocuted. We made the remainder of the trip without any more catastrophes. We used up a whole tank of gas, though it was only eighty miles round trip. We didn't know until we were loading up to go home, that Woody had traded the pigs for three gallons of moonshine. We had visited my Grandpa Sturgill, maybe three hours at the most, but Mom wanted to get back home before dark, if possible. So we loaded up, John and I once again in the dump bed, Mom, Woody and the two boys in the cab.

John and I were content until our dried fruit and cookies ran out, then we became bored. Sitting in the dump bed could be hazardous to your health. The bottom of the bed had a thin metal covering that helped the coal slide out better, but after a lot of use it would get little sharp metal pieces sticking up. One didn't want to be sitting down when Mom made one of her quick stops. So we spent most of our time standing up.

It was late evening when we made it back to the water trough. Mom wasted no time getting out of the truck and headed to the little house in the distance. Only this time, she was worried that dark was going to come before we got home. I looked after Jack and Jerry while Woody wandered off into the bushes. I could tell he had been into the moonshine. He was in a happy mood, but his hair was just starting to curl. Mom was back and fussing with us to get loaded up. Woody laughed at her and said, "Quit your worrying, we have head lights on the truck." The long day was taking its toll on Mom. She was tired and pale, all the way down to her knuckles, from squeezing the oversized steering wheel and I'm sure a lot of it was from Woody sipping on the gallon jug of white lightning. Three gallons were enough to stay drunk for three weeks or more. Woody tried to get Mom to take a drink, but she wisely refused.

Sometimes when Woody was in a good mood, he would let me take a drink. I didn't care much for beer, but acquired a liking for good moonshine. Here I was, 14 years old and already hooked on cigarettes and liked the taste of moonshine. This would be the case for many years of my life.

"Let's have one for the road," said Woody as he laid the gallon jug on his arm and took a big swallow. "Sure you don't want one?" But Mom only stared straight ahead with that worried look. Once again we all climbed aboard for the last few miles home. Mom must have forgotten to put the clutch in, because when she hit the button, the old truck fired in gear, making about ten jumps in a row before Mom could bring some control to it. John and I just about had our arms jerked out of their sockets from holding on. One thing we didn't want to do, was go sliding around on the back of that truck with that jagged metal bed. Job said in the Bible, "What I feared the most has come upon me." That must have been Mom's thoughts, because dark caught us long before we made it home.

Woody was right, there wasn't any need to worry because the headlights worked very well. With the motor revved up in second gear, the battery stayed in full charge. One could almost become hypnotized from looking in the ruts as we bounced and rocked the last two miles home. When Mom got out she said, "thank God we are home at last. I have never been so glad to see home."

Jack and Jerry both had fallen asleep, so Mom had John and I carry them up to the house. Woody said he was going to take his jugs of moonshine to the barn and hide it. He wasn't to the mean stage, yet. The girls came out in the yard and said they had been worried sick wondering what had happened to us, but Mom told them it was a long way over there and she was wore out and was going to get on home and rest. We got Jack and Jerry in the house and Mom said we had better get on back down to our house. I asked her if Woody was going to get mean and she said he was getting pretty sleepy and would probably come home and go to bed. When John and I got back down to our house, Woody was in the house and giving the girls a bad time. They later told me he had grabbed Evelyn and tried to get her in the bedroom and had torn her blouse. When John and I came, he started talking to us as the girls slipped quickly out into the night. Woody soon lost interest and said he better get on up to the house. After Woody left, the girls came back into the house. Although we spent a restless night, Woody didn't cause any trouble. He stayed drunk for a week and didn't eat anything for most of that time. He got so sick I thought he wasn't going to make it. He got the dry heaves, and would cough and gag until he would lose his breath and stop breathing. Finally his lungs would take in some air and he would go through the whole thing again. Woody sobered up for a couple days and finally got some food in him. He took a gallon of moonshine and sold it to his brother Pug.

Now Pug was twice as mean as Woody when he got drunk. Pug and his sister had been on the warpath with each other for a few days. She lived in a small house on their Dad's farm. She was a hard working- woman and expected others to do the same. She didn't like Pug living off their Mom and Dad and she was very bold in telling him so. As the story goes, Pug put a few drinks of moonshine in him, went over and torched her house, burning it to the ground. The story also goes that he laughed about it. He thought it was funny. She was smart, though. She took her three sons and left the area. Sometimes Pug would sit with his head down like he was sleeping and let out a yell "fire in the hole" and laugh and only he knew why.

Let me tell you a little bit of what it was like living next door to Pug. Twice he set his parent's house on fire. Once while they were working in the garden, they saw smoke coming from the house. They ran to the house to find Pug had piled wood in the middle of the living room and set it on fire. Another time he poured kerosene under his parents' bed and ignited it. Luckily they woke up before it was too late for them. They dragged the mattress outside, tried to beat the fire out, but too late. It had already done too much damage. It may have been beneficial to let the mattress burn and beat the fire out of Pug!

Are you getting the picture of how unsafe one could feel living close to Pug? Once there was a stray hound dog that took up residence at Pug's place (or rather his parents place, because he didn't own the clothes on his back,) but the dog wouldn't leave. Pug whipped it, threw rocks at it, so the story goes, but the dog came back, so Pug tied a baby diaper on the dog's tail, poured kerosene on the diaper and set it on fire. The old dog just stood there for a few seconds then realized that the burning diaper was tied to his tail. He took off running up the road past our house and headed across the field that was covered with dry grass a couple feet high. We lost sight of the dog, but we knew where he was by the way the smoke from the brush fire he was starting. It burned a twenty- acre field plus twice that in underbrush on our property and our neighbor's property.

No one carried insurance in those days, and Pug of course had zero funds. All Pug had to say was "now it's a doggone shame, ain't it?" All in all, the old field benefited from it and the underbrush was of no value except to us for hiding places. The dog didn't show up for more than a week. One morning the old dog went by our house on the way back to Pug's. He looked pretty bad, with the hair gone from his tail and part of his back parts. There were a lot of dried sores from the burns.

Growing up on a farm, I was used to killing animals, beef, pork, and chickens and it didn't bother me to shoot these animals. I also enjoyed hunting wild animals, but as I watched that old dog going back to what he felt was home, I felt a closeness and sadness for him. It reminded me of the plight of my family, how many times we had to run to keep from getting abused, physically, sexually and mentally. No one wanted to take in a half dozen kids. Most people were just about as poor as we were, so like the old dog, time after time, we would come sneaking back home with our tails between our legs, nervous and worried, yet having to take the chance things would be alright.

We needed food and we needed shelter, but what we needed more than any other thing was someone to love us, someone to put their arms around Evelyn, Wilma and Shirley without having sexual thoughts. Chuck, still a small boy, needed someone besides a big brother and sister to cuddle up to him by the evening fire, to read a book to him and let his mind travel to wherever the book would take him.

There isn't any way I can explain the hurt us older kids felt from the loneliness of the nights without the warmth of a fire, or an arm around you for comfort when you are sick and feverish, the hurt us older kids felt when we had to make the smaller ones be quiet when they were crying from hunger pangs, or were sick. It is the feeling that keeps cropping up when I see children mistreated and abused from parents who are alcoholics, or are on drugs. It's not the hunger pangs, nor the sleepless nights because of a fever. Those go away, but the wounds of the mind, the rejection, and the inner hurts of when your parents don't love you. These are the wounds that can't be treated with medicine, or food or a warm blanket. They are wounds that last a lifetime. It is the same thing that happens to a soldier seeing all the deaths in battle. The battle wounds on the physical body will heal, but the damage to the mind, the mental damage is like a thief. It will sneak up on you when you awaken in the night or when you least expect it. It will steal your joy and replace it with bitterness and hate. Why is there such cruelty in some people?

My mind goes back to the time when I watched a mule bleed to death in the same spot the dog is now standing. Our neighbors were moving from a small house they were renting to a larger house half a mile past our place. They had hooked a big, stout mule to a hay sled. These sleds are built long and have boards on them so one could stack dried loose hay on it. Here the reader may want to get a picture in his mind of a dog sled in the Alaska outback, but the hay sled is much larger. The sled was loaded with furniture above the sideboards.

The mule managed to pull the sled to our place, but he stopped to rest. His sides were heaving, so the man let the mule rest a minute or so then gave orders for the mule to pull, but the mule felt the load was too heavy and refused to pull anymore. The man started whipping him, but gained nothing. The mule tried a couple more times to move the sled, but to no avail.

Just a few feet past our store, three or four of us kids were playing. We watched nervously as the man took a butcher knife from the sled, walked up to the mule and slit it's throat. The blood came out in long squirts, splattering onto the sandy road, until there was a pool of blood. Its head began to get closer and closer to the ground until its knees gave way and it fell to the ground, dead in its own blood. The man had turned and walked away after he had cut its throat. Shirley and Chuck ran into the store where Mom was watching through the window. John and I walked over to see if we could do anything to help the mule, but there was nothing we could do. The sound that came from its breathing was a horrible gurgling, which stayed with me for years. John and I both had nightmares for months. The mule laid there for two or three hours before two men came by with a team of horses and drug the mule away and burned it.

There were some real mean, cruel people in the hill country. Some would and did, slit the throat of a man while on a hunting trip, walking away leaving him to bleed to death, much like the mule. He, like Pug, only spent a few years in prison, claiming self-defense.

I could tell about three more killings I knew about within a five-mile radius, but I don't see the need to do so. I just want the reader to understand why we felt helpless and scared to go to others for help. At the same time, there were people that loved and took good care of their family, but they weren't the norm.

Yes, at this time old dog and I had a lot in common. No one seemed to want us and we were both hungry, crying out to be loved, to have a gentle loving hand pat us on the head and say "you are a good boy," but instead we were doomed to go without food for the body or the soul.

A couple hours later Pug came by our house and wanted to know if there was any dynamite left from the mine. "Yes," I said "about half a case," and asked him how much he needed.

He said, "Oh, only 2 or three sticks."

"What do you need it for?" I asked.

"I'm going to blow a stump in the orchard."

"Can I come and watch? I'll stay out of the way."

"No, it's too dangerous," he said. "Them chunks fly a long way."

We went to the barn where we kept the dynamite and blasting caps. Pug cut off about eight feet of fuse. I told him that the fuse only burns two feet in a minute.

Pug said, "I know more about this than you do, Freddie". When Pug got out of site, I followed him. There was a fence running between our property and theirs, and there was a narrow strip of trees that had grown up around the fence. I sneaked up this fence line so I could see Pug blow the stump out. I felt safe under the small trees, but to my surprise, Pug had the old dog tied up in the orchard and was taping the dynamite around the dog's body. I thought he was going to blow the dog to pieces there in the orchard, but after he lit the fuse, he untied the dog and started throwing rocks at it. The old dog ran about fifty feet, stopped and stood looking back at Pug. All the cuss words and yelling didn't seem to bother the dog, but when the old dog looked back and saw the smoke from the burning fuse, he must have had a flash-back, because he headed down toward the creek and the howls could still be heard as he headed off up the mountain side. Pug was sitting on the stump laughing. I could see that his plan was to have the dog blow up out in the hills and no one would be the wiser, and it looked like that was going to happen. But it takes a long time for eight feet of fuse to burn up. Pug didn't know it, but I too was listening and waiting for the boom. But the laughing stopped as the howling started getting closer because the old dog had made a big circle and was headed back to where he felt was home. He ran past me and I have never seen such fear on an animal. His ears were laid back; his eyes were rolled back until only the whites were showing. He was so tired he could hardly keep going. He ran past Pug, who was throwing rocks at him and yelling, "Get back you dumb mangy hound," but the dog didn't even look up, just headed straight to Pug's house and ran under the porch. Most all the houses had porches on them. It was a gathering place after dinner for a place to sit and visit with the people passing by.

Well, as luck would have it, Pug's folks were sitting in their rocking chairs on the porch. When the old dog said goodbye to this world, he went out with a bang. It was an ear splitting boom. The old house shuddered, the windows were shattered and the boards from the porch blew all over the yard and out through the roof. Pug's Mom and Dad went flying through the air, though they weren't seriously hurt. They picked slivers out of their skin for days, and their hearing was never good after that. Of course there was dog meat scattered all over the place and it stunk for weeks. My intention isn't to make Pug look bad, but it gives the reader some insight into the conditions us kids were in.

Our food supply was exhausted and our income had vanished. My Dad had left some government bonds for us kids to go to college, but somehow they got cashed and spent.

Mom was true to her word and never drove the truck any more, but one day Woody got loaded on moonshine and decided he was going to learn to drive. He started the truck and took off, but he ran into the first culvert he came to, which was a real blessing, because he was still on our property. He bent the tie rod and did some other damage so the old truck was put out of commission.

We were only one of the many families going hungry in the Appalachians, as well as many other places in the forties. The government had to do something, so they started giving out commodities, war surplus foods, canned beef, cheese, beans and other surplus items. The county seat was seven miles away and that was where the food was distributed once every two weeks. We didn't have any transportation, so Mom had me go with her to help carry the food back. Woody was too proud and wouldn't go, so we left early with two- grain sacks, walked two miles to the main road, and caught a ride into the county seat. I was surprised to see so many people lined up for the free food. The line was over a block long. As we took our place in line, I could see Mom was embarrassed and I could see how worn and tired she had become. I have never had such troubled emotions. One part of me felt sorry for her and a deep love welled up in me for her and all the things we had been through these last two years, yet the other part of me hated her. I wanted to throw the grain sacks down and run and hide from it all.

We were surprised at how much food we received. The only questions they asked, were we living in the county and do you or your husband have a job and did we have any other means of making a living? Mom answered "No" but we both knew if we had worked the farm we could have had plenty. They loaded up our grain sacks and we hardly got out of sight when we started tearing off chunks of cheese and chewing on them. It was a long, tiring walk back home. We got a ride for a couple miles, but had to walk and carry the sacks of food the other five miles. We found out there was a bus that ran twice daily and we only had to walk two miles to and from the main road. After a trip or two it got to be routine and we were soon looking forward to visiting with the other people while standing in line.

So once again we adjusted to fit the circumstances. I have heard many a military man complain about the chip beef on toast, the Spam and powdered milk, but to us kids it was like a king's banquet. There wasn't one morsel left, nor was there one complaint.

It has been many years since this happened. The dates and in some cases the seriousness is gone from my mind. I'm not so concerned about the accuracy of the time that it happened, but the facts of what happened. I think it was early spring that Woody had been on a two or three day drunk, and he and his brother-in law had been in a fight with each other. The brother-in-law had used a pair of steel knuckles to work Woody over. Woody stayed in our house and the girls cleaned up his forehead, which had a couple good gashes in it. But he wasn't hurt so bad that it stopped his sex glands from working. He kept trying to cop a feel when the girls got within reach. We all went out on the front porch just as Woody's brother-in-law was headed into our place. Woody's mother came running up the road, getting there just in time to stop another fight. She gathered her son-in-law by the shirt and headed him back toward home. Mom heard the yelling and cussing and came down to get Woody. He was still mad and wanted to go back to his mother's place and have another go at his brother-in-law, but his mother came back and between her and Mom, they got him to go home and sleep it off.

Things calmed down until late afternoon. I was chopping firewood, when I heard Mom scream out like she was in pain. I looked up and about half way between their house and ours, Mom was trying to tear her-self away from Woody. He had her by the hair and was beating her in the face. As she fell backwards from the blow, she fell into a huge patch of blackberry briars. The briars were five or six feet tall and had huge thorns on them. Mom was trying to crawl into the briars to escape. Having long black hair, she had become a helpless prisoner of the briars. Her dress was also tangled and she was lying there helpless as Woody started kicking her. I became so angry, that I ran into the house and grabbed a twenty-two rifle that I hunted with, looking frantically for shells. I could only find one, but I felt that it would be enough. I quickly loaded the gun and ran back to where Mom was now pleading with Woody to get her out of the briars. The pitiful moans coming from Mom made me even more determined to put an end to this problem and the problem was now standing only ten feet in front of me. I raised the rifle and took careful aim between his eyes and I can still hear my mother's voice ringing in my ears. "No, son, don't do it please, don't do it."

I had no doubt that when the gun went off, Woody would go down just like the hogs I shot between the eyes at butchering time. When I pulled the trigger, instead of an explosion, I heard a loud click. Never before had the gun failed to fire. I was more shocked than my step dad. I cocked the gun, aimed and pulled the trigger again, only to hear the same click. Never in my life have I felt more frustrated than I was at that minute. I ejected the shell, picked it up and examined it. There was a groove in it showing that the firing pin was working. I inserted the shell once again, raised the gun and aimed once more. For the first time I saw fear on Woody's face. He said, "Fred, you stop that silliness" and for the third time I pulled the trigger. All that happened was a loud click once again. At that sound, I just couldn't handle it anymore. My step dad just turned and walked away, unconcerned. My Mom was still lying in the briar patch, crying. I sat down beside her, and with my heart breaking I cried with her, with a heaviness that no young person should ever have to bear. I have never felt so helpless and defeated. I cried out to God, asking Him why He would let this happen to any family.

I don't want to give the impression that I was the only one carrying a heavy burden. My brother and sisters had gotten there and slowly we cut away hair, dress and briars. Finally we got Mom out and took her and the boys, Jack and Jerry, home with us. Mom looked awful for a few days. Some of the briars had broken off, were hard to get out and had become infected.

After a week Woody came by and wanted Mom to come back home with him, but she seemed determined that this time she wasn't going back. Shirley and Chuck were very excited about their mother being home. They couldn't get enough of sitting in her lap.

A man came by one day and told Mom she had to pay back the government a lot of money. Unknown to us, Mom had been getting a Social Security check from the government and though Evelyn had turned eighteen some months before, Mom had kept drawing money for her. Mom told the man she thought as long as Evelyn was living at home, she had a right to claim her. The man was very patient explaining to Mom that she had broken the law and could actually go to jail.

Mom started calling on God again and this time he might have heard her. The man listened as Mom explained how poor we were and had no way of paying it back. The man only had to look around at the worn out furnishings, the scrawny kids all over the place, Mom with half of her hair chopped off and her face, still showing all the battle wounds. The government man told Mom he was going to cancel the debt, but when the other kids turned eighteen, they would have to be taken off Social Security. Mom wished a hundred blessings upon the man with the promise that she would never make that mistake again.

After the man left, we asked Mom what all the money had been spent for. She answered, "Well I guess it went for school clothes and food." I guess when you are young, things like that just skip your mind, but I just can't remember much food; or clothes either. I have wondered how much money she got a month for us kids. I have even wanted to research it.

Woody started coming by the house more often. He was living back home with his folks. He let Mom know that he was working in a coal mine about two miles away and was making about nine dollars a day and he wanted her to come back home. "I am home," she said "and that's the way it's going to stay." But one evening he stopped by on his way home from work. Like before, he would sit on the porch and talk to Mom through the screen door.

"I've worked hard all day long and walked two miles from the job and I'm starved to death. You could at least bring me a bowl of beans." Yep, you guessed it. Mom took Woody a plate of food.

"Well, you are going to have to change this and change that," I heard Mom telling Woody. He must have agreed because the next day Mom took Jack and Jerry and moved back in with him. It was really hard on Shirley and Chuck and really on all of us when she went back to him. It caused another low spot in our life.

Things actually were quite peaceful for a while. Woody had only been drinking beer on weekends, but one night about ten o'clock, I heard Wilma cussing and screaming. John and I ran to find Woody with his pants down and trying to get in bed with Wilma. She surprised me with all the new cuss words she had learned. John ran into the kitchen and grabbed a butcher knife. I think John would have run it through him if we would have let him. I think Woody thought so too, for he had zipped his pants up and out the door he went. The next day Wilma told Mom what he had done and I suspect this is what brought about the next big change in our lives. Less than a week later, early Saturday morning, a dump truck or coal truck as we called them, pulled up to our front door. Woody and Mom came down and without explaining or giving any reason told us we were moving to Virginia. We just stood there in total shock. We all said we weren't going.

Mom said "don't you tell me what you aren't going to do." She gave us orders to get our clothes in a sack and help load the furniture and in less time than it takes to order and eat a Big Mac at Mc Donald's, the furniture was stacked and tied down in the truck.

CHAPTER 3

Moving To Virginia

Our furniture consisted of the very basics. For the living room we had one very worn couch and two chairs; one kitchen table, with four wooden homemade chairs and a bench, a few pots and pans, dishes, four beds and blankets for each bed, no extras of anything. Somehow they managed to get the mattresses stacked so we could sit on them. One part of me would have given thousands to have had a picture of us nine kids plus the old white dog, Bingo, yet the other part of me couldn't bear to look at the picture if I had one.

There is one thing that will never leave me. That is the fear of the unknown and the agony of leaving the place where I was born and grew up. Even though there was a lot of heartache and sorrow, there were also lots of good memories. There was the security of knowing the mountains, every trail, creek and stream, knowing I could live off the land if I had to. Now we were going to another state, new school, new teachers that knew nothing about us.

Woody's friend who owned the truck, Mom, Woody and the baby, Jerry rode in the cab. The other eight of us, including the old dog, were in the back, everyone trying to find a comfortable place to sit as the old coal truck started making it's way down the bumpy, dirt road to the highway, which was two miles away.

Usually us kids would be talking with each other, but today there was an unusual quietness about us as we passed our neighbors farm, past the little two-room schoolhouse that taught from first through eighth grade. Most of the kids received a good education, but there were a few like me that would go through many years of their life paying the penalty for not having enough education. All of our eyes were focused on what we were leaving behind. Our old home place, our neighbors and the old school house, faded into the distance.

One would think we would have been glad to go, leaving a place where there had been so many heartaches and sorrows, fear and sleepless nights, and hunger. But above all, our hearts were filled with hate and bitterness. But I would have gone back, gladly instead of the unknown in Virginia. We wouldn't make eye contact with each other because we knew the tears were ready to erupt.

Just before we got to the highway, I looked upon the hill where my father was buried and once again felt mad at him for leaving us. I was mad at Mom, Woody, and God, but most of all, at myself. I couldn't hold back the wall of tears anymore, so I turned my head away so no one could see, and I let the flood of tears loose. I suspect some of the other kids were doing the same thing. When the truck got to the highway and picked up speed, the coal dust which hadn't been washed out kept swirling around and soon the small kids had their eyes full of coal dust and were crying. By the time we got to the dirt road, that would take us up to the farm, we were all streaked with black coal dust and tears. As we bounced our way over a mile of bad road on top of the now filthy mattresses, I can only imagine what our appearance looked like. Probably somewhat like or worse than the transient people in the movie "The Grapes of Wrath."

We became eager to see the farm. I had been here with Dad shortly after he bought the place. It seemed big and overpowering to my young eyes and was half a mile to our nearest neighbor. It sat in a big valley and was enclosed by a mountain which we called the mouth. The only way into the valley was in the direction we were going. The mouth was about two hundred yards wide, making our farm very private. The ridges were covered with commercial size timber. Dad had also bought the mineral rights with the place in case there was coal or oil underneath. He had logged some of the smaller trees, which he used to build a log barn and also had some logs sawed and had built a small two- bedroom house. For a time he had rented it out to share croppers. The place looked real good with its green valley and beautiful rhodo-dendrons. Its peacefulness captured my spirit right off and I could see John was feeling the same way.

We baled out of the truck and into the house to get a look at our new home. It was no more than eight or nine hundred square feet. The living room and kitchen had the only furnish-ings, a wood cook stove in the kitchen and a pot bellied coal or wood stove in the living room. They both looked well used and lonesome, but that would soon change. As we started bringing in the furniture, Mom had me gathering wood so she could start preparing a meal. Wood was plentiful and it wasn't long before the old cook stove was heating up. The pipes were rusted and had small holes and puffs of smoke were pushing out of the holes, but no one paid much attention to it. The next day they were replaced. In short order the beds were set up including one in the living room.

Woody and the trucker were headed back to Kentucky for a load of coal and a plow, but they wouldn't be back today. After dinner we all pitched in and cleaned things up somewhat, but there was still coal dust on every thing. Mom released John and I to explore the valley. She was worried we may get lost and told us to stay close by, but that was asking too much. We took off like young horses out of a barn. We checked the creek for fish and the hills for squirrels and rabbits. We came dragging in shortly before dark, to a warm house and a worried mother. But John and I had gotten acquainted with a big part of the valley and in that short time the land came to welcome us and we accepted the invite.

As dark settled in, we all sat on the porch and talked about a lot of things, about school and farming. Mom said Woody was going to stay in Kentucky and work, be home weekends and she was going to be here with us. She had big plans for the farm and said as a family we could make a good living off of it. We all got caught up in the excitement of it.

We sat there in the warmth of the spring night, listening to the whippoorwill calling, and the trickle of the small creek making music as it moved over the rocks and pebbles, finding it's way out of the valley, like it had been doing for thousands of years.

I can still see the stars playing hide and seek with the clouds. The only thing that could have been any more relaxing would have been the southern fire flies. They would be coming in about another month. But tonight was plenty good enough. Even the small kids seemed to understand this was a special night. They were very quiet as we all huddled together, letting the love for each other and the tranquility of the night have its way. Sleepiness and tiredness finally took over and John and I went to bed on a mattress still covered with coal dust, but that was no problem. We talked about how frightened we were when we left Kentucky that morning and how happy and excited we were to be here. We went to sleep listening to a pair of red foxes barking from on top of the ridge and it gave us a good feeling to know we had been on that ridge just hours ago. We went to sleep in total contentment.

Early next morning, John and I were eager to eat and go back and finish our exploring, but Mom had other plans for us. There was a covered shed by the house and Mom wanted

John and I to start stacking wood in it. We burned coal ninety percent of the time, but you had to start a fire with wood first, then put blocks of coal on it. We were glad when Woody and his friend showed up with the load of coal about ten o'clock. He had about fifty pounds of seed potatoes, plus seed beans and corn. They had also brought a plow, along with shovels and hoes. There was a trail that went through the mountains that had been hacked out by the Indians and settlers, and it was only about twenty miles by horseback to our Kentucky farm. I later made that trip two or three times.

Woody said a young man was going to be bringing a mule over in a couple of days and he was kidding Evelyn about keeping the handsome young man there. She told him to hush, she didn't need a man, but I could see she was looking forward to seeing what he looked like. To my knowledge, she had not been on a date since her husband Bill had left and I'm sure she wanted a life of her own. She had taken over as mother to us and she seemed determined to stay the course. Mom sent John and I to our neighbors to buy two frying chickens. We saw the chickens running loose when we came in the day before. Mom gave me four quarters and said if they were over fifty cents each, just get one. Now this seems like it would be the simplest thing to do, but we were both frightened and it was probably the slowest half a mile I ever walked. We explored every track we saw in the sandy soil.

The coon tracks were the most interesting. They looked like a baby's foot and when we found a track we couldn't identify, we let our imagination take over. Sometimes I would get lost in a dream world.

When we got to the path leading up to the farmhouse, we saw a middle age woman working in a berry patch. This made us a little more relaxed. She spotted us, stood up and adjusted her apron and bonnet, then put her hand over her eyes, shading them from the sun. She waited patiently while we made the last hundred yards last as long as we could.

"You must be them new people up the holler," she said.

"Yes we are," I mumbled, shaking my head up and down. "My mom wanted to know if you would sell us a frying chicken for dinner."

"Well, yes, but I think they're getting too big for fryers. The roosters are twenty five cents each and the hens are gonna be laying before long. I'll have to charge you thirty cents a piece for them."

"Two roosters will be fine," I said, and gave her two quarters. She went into the shed and came out with a handful of grain. She yelled "here chick-chick" and chickens came running from out of the tall grass, the chicken house and from underneath the house within seconds. There were fifty or more chickens. She took a long wire with a hook on one end, reached out and hooked it around a chicken's leg and in less than thirty seconds we had two of the biggest frying chickens I had ever seen. She let us know she was a widow lady and she made her living selling chickens, eggs, berries, milk and fresh vegetables in the fall. She said she took care of everything herself except the plowing. Her brother, who lived the next place over, took care of that. I looked at the well cared for place, though it was old and unpainted. Everything she needed was there. A short ways from the house was a small barn and another small building close to it. I could hear squeals coming from there and from this I could tell there was more than one hog. For a minute I felt lonesome for the farm we left in Kentucky, where my dad had supported us very good and through the store had met the needs of other families.

The half a mile back home went very quickly as John and I talked about making this farm just as productive as the widow lady, Boggs' place; but that was just one more dream that never materialized. Mom was happy with the two chickens. She said she had never seen fryers so big and wished we would have gotten four of them. In less time than it would take for me to tell you, Mom had the roosters beheaded and in a pot of boiling water to remove the feathers.

Before Woody left for Kentucky, he picked out two or three acres for the garden and wanted John and I to get started plowing as soon as the mule got there. About noon the second day after Woody left, a tall lanky man, about twenty years old came riding up to the house on a beautiful black horse and following behind him on a lead rope was a big mule. Mom went out and talked to the man. I was soon called out to take the mule to the barn. The man said the mule's name was Jim. He already had the harness on and was ready to hook to a plow, but Mom said to wait until morning.

When I got back from the barn, the man was at the table eating. He and Evelyn kept glancing at each other, but as far as I know they never spoke. Mom told the man he was welcome to stay the night. "Well, thank you, ma'am for the invite and for the food, but I want to be on the other side of the mountain before dark." With that he climbed aboard the shiny black horse and rode off into the sunset and we never saw him again.

John and I were up early and all excited about plowing, but Mom said John had to clean out the spring for the drinking water. It had gotten filled up with silt. We had been using water from the creek, but now with animals walking through it and drinking from it, we needed to start using the spring. It wasn't going to be as much fun by myself. I soon had Jim harnessed up and hooked to the plow and it was exciting to be the first one to sink a plow in our new garden. Jim wasn't a stranger to a plow. He knew what to do and in a few minutes, we had our first pass across the field. I had new hope well up in me as I saw the good loamy soil being turned over.

Even though it was a month late for putting in a garden, I felt with the rich new ground, we could still have a good crop. Shortly after daylight the next morning Mom shook me awake.

My body ached from the hard work and already the fun and excitement had departed from me. All that was left was a tired, aching body with sore muscles. After a long week of plowing, old Jim and I were both ready to retire as farmers.

Woody was real pleased with all we had gotten done and I was glad for his help in putting in the rows. Although I was improving, it was easy to tell my crooked rows from his straight ones. The whole family was planting and hoeing. Mom was planting the seed potatoes, John was planting the vegetable seed, Wilma and I were fertilizing and covering the seeds, Woody was at the plow and Evelyn was looking after the small kids and cooking.

We were more than glad when the last row of corn was covered. We were both tired and proud as we looked over at the long week's work and headed toward the house, sweaty but happy. Evelyn had a big pot of soup beans and cornbread ready. We would have made any cook happy for there wasn't a morsel of food left when we got through. We ate enough for a dozen people; but then we were almost a dozen people.

The night had already closed in on us. Once again we were all on the front porch except Evelyn and Wilma who were doing the dishes by a coal oil lamp. All the time we were there the power was never hooked up. The meter had been taken off the house and had never been replaced. But tonight that wasn't a problem. We were a family. Mom and Woody were laughing and having fun and it was a perfect night in my memory.

Woody left the next morning for Kentucky. He walked down to the little country store and caught the bus. I hated to see him go. It was good to have a man around so I didn't have to make decisions, and Woody was a good guy when he was sober. Mom sent John and me back to the widow Boggs' place to buy five laying hens. The people that had lived there before had built a terrible chicken house with a very small fenced in yard. We put the hens in it with some` grain and they were a little nervous for a couple minutes then started eating. The next day they went right to work with five big brown eggs.

Mom had us kids wash up and get our best clothes on. We had to sign up for school for the following year. There was only two days left until summer vacation. We all felt like a fish out of water. We didn't know anyone and we were all so bashful. Our face would turn beet red if someone would speak to us. We were supposed to have our last year's report card when we left Kentucky, but none of us had gotten them. Mom told the teacher she would have them before school started. I knew I wouldn't pass this year. My grades were D and F. (The D, because they had hopes for me or they were trying to encourage me.) I knew it wasn't because I deserved it. But Mom put me in a higher grade and gave me a warning; I had better do good and not embarrass her. That probably did more damage to me than any other thing. If I had taken the same grade over again, I might have caught up but even though I tried hard and wanted to do good, I kept sliding further behind until I lost all hope and quit trying.

I'm glad I didn't know what the future held for us. We left school and stopped at the Mullins Country Store, the one where Woody had caught the bus. We got some groceries, also some grain for the mule and the chickens. Mom opened up a charge account. The lady running the store was Orrie Mullins, the owner. She would play an important part in my life in the future. She had six kids, all about our age. We would later become good friends. I was going to bring the mule down to haul back the grain, but Orrie said that wouldn't be neces- sary; her oldest son would bring it up in the pickup when he got home from school. It was about a mile to our house, all up hill and we had only been home a few minutes when Bill Mullins came roaring up to our place in an International truck. He had the hundred pound sack of grain and also had the three younger kids with him. Bill was about eighteen and his brother J.D. was sixteen, and two of his sisters, Judy, was my age and Carrie, was John's age. How good can it get? They were all very friendly and very talkative, but as usual John and I were red faced and quiet. Bill said our farm was called Meadow Branch Farm and we always referred to it as that. J.D. asked me if he could come up and hunt on our place. I told him he could and we became instant friends. My heart leaped every time I looked at Judy. She was very beautiful with long black hair and big sparkling brown eyes.

The following Saturday, Woody and his trucker friend came in. Woody brought two young pigs and a roll of block wire or hog wire as it was called. He had John and me digging postholes, while he and his friend harnessed up the mule and cut down some small trees and made them into fence posts. We soon had a small pigpen fenced in, not pretty to look at, but it was tough. We took on the appearance of being real farmers. We even acquired a milk cow, but not a very good one. She was a cross breed of a white face and probably Jersey, more of a beef stock, but gave about a gallon of milk a day. We were hungry for milk and butter. That was only a glass a day each. The garden was doing good but the hoeing and weeding were hard work, so we didn't work it as often as we should have.

We had made friends with a family that lived pretty close to the country store. Their life story was a lot like ours. Their name was Holley and their Dad was an alcoholic. His only income was when someone would bring a car that needed work on. He would work all day for a jug of whiskey and twenty five cents for a few groceries. They mostly lived off the land and some of their family would drop off a few groceries now and then. Their oldest son, Clyde was the same age as Evelyn. One day, Evelyn and I went to the store and she and Clyde started looking at each other. They seemed to like what they saw, so a couple days later Clyde showed up at our place riding a bicycle and according to him, was just out for a ride and ended up here.

Well, that bicycle seemed to end up there two or three times a week. Although Clyde had been out of school three or four years, he had not been able to find a job, so he spent most of his time hanging out at the store or helping his dad tinker on cars and later became a pretty fair mechanic.

Two weeks went by and Woody had not shown up and Mom was getting worried. We had no phone and no way of contacting him, so Mom decided to take the bus to Kentucky to find out what happened to him. She put a few things in a paper bag, saying she would be back the next day. Wilma and I walked with her to the country store and Orrie said there was a letter there that had just come in for Mom. We went out and sat down on the steps of the store and Mom's hand was shaking when she opened the letter. Mom read it two or three times before telling us that Woody and Pug had been on a three day drunk and Woody had fallen and broke his leg, was in a cast and on crutches.

The bus was due in about an hour so Mom made the decision to go back home and get more stuff. We almost ran that mile back home. She quickly threw a few more things together and got Jack and Jerry and we headed back down the road to the store. She would probably be gone two or three days, she said as she boarded the bus. She gave us a bunch of orders, like to not spend our time playing, make sure the animals got fed and to not let the weeds take over the garden.

We watched as the smoky, smelly bus drove off down the gravel road and out of sight. We already felt scared and lonely, and with heads down, we started that mile walk back home. Days came and went without any news from Mom and Woody. Wilma had met a girl her age that lived on a farm about a half mile away. Their last name was Church. As the days passed by, Wilma started spending two or three days at a time with the Church's. Occasionally she would bring homemade candy and cookies to us. Wow what a treat!

Three weeks went by. We didn't know what to do. Orrie said our grocery bill had to be paid. We now had chickens, pigs, a cow and a mule to feed and costing just about as much to feed them as it did us. John and I were both hooked on cigarettes and J.D. our friend, who's Mom owned the store, would steal tobacco for us and we learned how to roll our own. A bag of tobacco only cost about five or ten cents, but we weren't allowed to charge anything but groceries and animal food.

Thank God, Woody and Mom showed up. We were both mad and glad. Mom said Woody hadn't been able to take care of himself and she felt we would be all right. "I just did what I thought was the best thing to do. It took time to rent out the small house and get the new renters moved in."

What bothered us more than anything was they had left Jack and Jerry with Woody's Mom and Dad. His cast was off but he was still using crutches. His brother-in-law, who had brought them, was unhappy because the road was so rough. He was driving the most beautiful car I had ever seen. It was shiny black, almost like looking into a mirror and had lots of chrome. He was crawling under the car checking his oil pan and said he wasn't ever going to bring his car up that road again. He was from Detroit, Michigan and wasn't used to these kinds of roads. He was eager to get back down out of these mountains.

Within the hour they were headed back down the valley, Mom giving orders for all the things to do. She was going to pay the grocery bill and wanted us to stop spending so much. She said she wouldn't be gone very long this time. So once again we watched them go out of sight. Shirley and Chuck were crying and I was feeling mad and depressed.

The fall colors were getting more brilliant each day. There were so many varieties of hardwoods and it made the valley look like a post card. School was a disaster. John and I skipped more days than we went. The Holley boys were usually with us. I had already given up thinking of trying to catch up. I should have been held back two grades but no one seemed to care if we were in school or not. I felt the same way.

Another month went by without seeing Mom and Woody. The crops were getting ready to harvest. We had been enjoying the fresh corn, beans, and tomatoes. The beans had done really good, the tomatoes fair, the ears of corn were small, but tasted good. It would have done much better if we had spent more time working the garden and less time hunting and playing. I think that is about the time I realized this could be a prosperous farm with the right family. But regretfully we would never be that family. My spirit sank as I realized mine or my father's dreams were never going to be reached.

Mom and Woody showed up with canning jars. The new renter had a panel truck and both doors in the back opened up. It was the ideal vehicle for that country. It had two large seats and also had lots of room for cargo. They were all going to stay for a couple days and help get the crops harvested.

Mom and the girls took care of the canning. Woody, John, the renter and me took care of getting the crops harvested and ready for drying, pickling and canning. Evelyn and Wilma had already canned about 20 gallons of sauerkraut before Mom got there. I can't remember how we got the jars, maybe from the Church's where Wilma spent a lot of time. The old cook stove was going from daylight until dark, with the big canning tub boiling. Mom would stoke the fire just before going to bed and the tub of water would still be real warm when she got out of bed the next morning. By daylight she would be putting another twenty jars in to cook.

Woody had plowed up the potatoes and it was fun to watch them pop out of the ground. They had probably done better than the other crops. It was back breaking work. They had to be picked up and put into a bucket or basket and carried and put in piles to dry for a couple days. It's amazing how much food can be raised on two acres. The kitchen was stacked three feet high with jars of vegetables plus two fifteen gallon crocks of pickled beans and corn mixed together. After the jars would cool, they would be transported to the front porch to make room for the next batch. One had to be careful when taking jars out of the boiling water. If the air was too cool, the jars would break. It did require some skill.

After the potatoes got dry, Woody had John and I start putting them into sacks and they would drive the panel as close as they could to them. In those days the horse and cow feed came in sacks, also the chicken feed, flour and beans, so we had a variety pack from twenty five to one hundred pound sacks to put the potatoes in.

Woody and the renter drove out of the valley and were gone for three or four hours. When they got back they were both drinking and had a big handsome man with them. His name was Max. He said he was going to take Max up to the head of the farm and show Max some trees he wanted logged. I wanted to go with them but he wouldn't let me. This seemed strange to me because I knew where every merchantable-tree lived and probably the best way to get them out, but Woody was very firm and said "no" and gave me a bunch of chores to do. I was hurt and disappointed. Outwardly I was being obedient and started doing the chores, but inside I was cussing and screaming and took my frustration out on John and the other kids. Even the old dog didn't want to be around me.

It was late when Woody got back to the house. He and Mom were doing a lot of whispering. It was easy to tell something was going on that us kids weren't supposed to know about. The next morning was departure time for Woody and the renter. We stacked sacks of potatoes and over a hundred quart jars of canned goods. The panel truck was a stout built truck but it was squatting when they left the farm. Woody and the renter both had headaches and didn't eat breakfast but came in for a cup of coffee before heading out for Kentucky, saying they would be back tomorrow for another load.

About ten o'clock the next morning, they drove into the yard and in short order we were loading more produce in the panel. They had brought lots of boxes for the canned goods. Some jars had busted in yesterdays move and Mom wasn't too happy about that. She blamed it on the driver for being drunk, but the roads were so rough we were lucky to lose only a couple jars.

After a quick lunch, the truck was loaded and once again our heart sank when we realized Mom was going back to Kentucky again. "It will only be for a few days," Mom said as she stuffed a few clothes in the back seat, which was loaded with potatoes. Woody was holding Jack, and Mom was holding Jerry; the panel truck groaned as it crept down the narrow dirt road, leaving us once again, like orphans to make it on our own.

It was two months before they showed up again. It was now late fall and the weather was cold. Our coal supply was down to a few buckets. We only built a fire in the cook stove to conserve fuel. We stayed bundled up and spent most of our time around the kitchen stove, so we were very glad to see a coal truck come in and back up to our coal pile; or where it had been. There were a couple tons of good block coal, not enough to last through the long winter, but when you are down to your last bucket, two ton looks like a forever supply.

My happiness was short lived when I discovered Mom and the boys weren't with Woody and he was quick to let us know that Mom and the boys were ok. He said Mom wasn't feeling very good, and thought she had the flu. Woody and the trucker wandered up the valley. Woody said he was going to show the trucker our farm. I started to come along, but once again he wouldn't let me go with them. I became suspicious there was something out of the ordinary going on in the upper valley and I was determined to find out what it was. After he went back to Kentucky, I was going to hike back in there and look around. When Woody and the trucker got back, they had been drinking and had a couple pints in their pockets. I thought they had walked over the hill to the Hampton farm on the other side of the hill and bought the moonshine, although I wondered why they hadn't driven around with the truck. I soon lost all interest in the "whys" as I realized Woody was going to stay with us a couple days. The old fear returned and I could feel my heart pounding; I could sense the fear in the other kids.

It had been drizzling rain off and on and was now turning to light snow. John and I grabbed the coal buckets and went out to get the night's coal in before the pile got covered with snow, but what we really wanted was to make a plan of what we should do about Woody. The trucker was in a hurry to get going before the snow started sticking. They had a farewell drink with each other and the trucker started cranking the engine but the battery was low and cold and refused to start. He let it set there for a few minutes and tried again but the battery was just too weak to start the engine. The trucker started cussing the truck, the snow and a whole bunch of other things he wasn't happy with; like spending the night in this cold miserable place. Woody decided to get the mule and pull the truck to start it. While Woody was getting the mule hitched up, me and the other kids were begging God to not let the truck start so we wouldn't be there by ourselves with Woody.

The ground was muddy and wet from the drizzle. With the mule pulling and us bigger kids pushing, the tires would just slide when the trucker would let out the clutch. The road had deep ruts and the truck was just more than the mule could pull. So he, being smarter than us, quit trying. This made Woody and the trucker very frustrated. We had only moved the truck about fifty feet. Old Jim was also frustrated. He would just lunge into the rigging but not really pulling. Woody went over and broke a large limb off a tree and started whipping the mule. The mule was getting nervous and upset and he started rearing up. This seemed to be more than he could take and walked in front of the mule and started beating him in the face. One of the limbs caught him in the eye and white milky substance squirted out. For months I relived that scene. I would wake up at night and see the old mule turning his head in pain, chewing and popping his teeth. If ever there was an animal that cried that old mule did. Tears ran down his face and he let out a mule bray that was the most sorrowful thing I have ever heard.

I could see it bothered Woody and the trucker. He was sorry for what he'd had done. He unhooked him and said for me to get the lazy worthless mule back to the barn. John and I took old Jim back to the barn. We took the rigging off and tried to clean his eye out. There was just a deep socket left. There wasn't any doubt old Jim was blind in the right eye. From that day on, we gave him the name "Blind Jim." One had to be careful how you approached him. It had to be from the good eye side or he may run over you.

It was almost dark when we got back to the house and was almost freezing out. Evelyn and Wilma had dinner ready. The trucker had drained the radiator in the truck and was still complaining about having to stay the night. He and Woody were still drinking and picking at each other. It had caused friction in the house because Evelyn and Wilma were also picking at each other. We were hoping that Woody wouldn't try anything with the girls while the trucker was there. Evelyn fixed a pallet on the floor for the man, Woody slept on the couch. Although we were all tense when the lantern was turned off, the night passed without any problem. The trucker was up and had a fire going at daylight. The ground was frozen and it felt like it had froze in the house, but the water bucket had no ice in it. That was our only gauge of how cold it was. The trucker said he was cold all night. The only thing that separated him from the ground was one- inch tongue and groove flooring with no insulation.

While Evelyn was cooking breakfast, John and I went to the barn to feed and check on the mule. The eye had lots of dried stuff on it, and it must have been sore for he didn't like me cleaning it, but I managed to clean it up some. John and I talked about killing Woody, but we didn't like the thoughts of going to jail. We considered rat poison again but we didn't have any D-Con or money to buy it with. We were hoping Woody would go back to Kentucky today and we wouldn't have to worry about it.

The sun came out and thawed the ground, making the clay ground muddy. It stuck to our shoes like glue. The battery in the truck had a little power in it, but not enough to start the truck, so they took it out and put it in a grain sack and carried it a mile to Holley's garage and got it charged. By mid morning they were back and put water in the truck, hooked up the battery and the truck fired right up. Our heart sank as the trucker drove off and left Woody. We were all real quiet around the lunch table. Woody tried to be funny, but it was hard to laugh. After lunch, he walked off toward the barn and was gone for a couple hours. I walked up to see what he was doing and saw his tracks going back into the woods and heading up the valley. Late evening Woody showed up real drunk. As Job said "the thing I feared the most has come upon me."

We had been discussing what to do if Woody came in drunk. As usual we did a lot of talking, but didn't come up with any solutions. We fell back to what had always worked in the past and that was to run and hide if we had to. The weather was cold and off and on snowflakes were falling. We would have to find a barn with hay so we could crawl in and stay warm.

The neighbor whose farm joined ours had a big barn. It was close to a mile away, but we felt this would be our best bet. Evelyn and Wilma lingered in the kitchen washing the dishes and cleaning up. I could feel their nervousness, as they were snappy with each other. Shirley was putting heavy nightgowns on Chuck and Phyllis in case we had to leave the house. Woody had lain down on the couch and was snoring. I kept thinking about stabbing him with a butcher knife. One part of me just couldn't do it, yet another part of me wanted to. I guess I didn't have the killer instinct, or maybe it was fear. But the main reason, I really did like Woody. It was just easier to run.

All the chores were done; kindling wood for the cook stove was brought in. Once again it was decision time. Do we go or stay? Woody was still snoring. He had consumed a lot of whiskey, so we thought or more than that, hoped, he would sleep all night. We decided to push the two beds together and shove them against the wall. All the girls got in the back against the wall and John, Chuck, and I in the outer bed. It was crowded but that wasn't a big problem. We sat a chair in the doorway so it would tip over if it got bumped. We hoped this would wake us up. I had an old army dagger that I put under my pillow and hoped I wouldn't have to use it.

I don't know how long I had been sleeping when the chair fell, making a noise. I'm sure we all woke up. Though it was a dark winter night, I could make out Woody as he slowly came up to the bed. His hand went under the blanket. I could almost see the shock of disappointment on his face when he found only male parts. He reached on past me, finding John; he jerked his hand back and said, "What the----?" He stood there for a few seconds, and then left the room cussing. I got up and put the chair back up for a signal in case he came back again, but he didn't return.

John and I got up at daylight and got the fire going in the cook stove. At the same time Woody had gotten up and started a fire in the living room stove. The warmth would feel good when I came back in from the outside, from draining my bladder. The ground was frozen solid and I thanked God for not having to spend the night out doors. As I approached the house, I could see Evelyn through the window. She had lit the lantern and was starting breakfast when Woody came up behind her, grabbed her breast with one hand and between the legs with the other. She let out a scream. I rushed through the door yelling at Woody to let her go, which he did. He laughed and said, "I thought you were your mother."

"You do that again, and I will pour hot grease over you," Evelyn said.

"Well, you look a lot like your mother," he said as he walked into the living room. There was a fruit house about fifty feet from the house. We had the jars of canned food and potatoes in it. Some of the jars had ice in them, though none had broken. John and me cut straw and covered everything, including the potatoes, which were in a bin. We hadn't been to school and this made Woody mad, not because we needed an education, but because he was hoping Evelyn would be there by herself. He was irritable all morning and was starting to hit the bottle again. We were kept busy cutting wood and any other chore he could find. I suspect he was going to work us so hard we would be glad to go to school tomorrow.

After lunch, we kids decided we were going to get out before dark when Woody laid down for a nap, which he did when he was drinking. When we left, Wilma would go to the Church's, where she spent a lot of time, John and I would go to the Mullins, Evelyn, Shirley and Phyllis would stay with Clyde Sturgill's family, Evelyn's boyfriend. Chuck would go with John and me. We didn't know if they would have room for us, but like I said desperate people do desperate things.

There isn't anyway I can explain the happiness that came over us when we saw our mother coming toward the house. She was carrying an old worn suitcase that looked just about as tired as she did. We probably looked like we were going to stampede her as we rushed out to meet her. She looked all haggard and worn. There wasn't any happiness showing in her. She never asked if we were all right but wanted to know if Woody was there. "He was supposed to come back with the trucker," she said. "What has he been doing?" she asked, looking at me.

"Causing trouble," I said with tears in my eyes. "He tried to get in bed with the girls." Mom's face went white and I went on to tell her how he tried to get in bed with them and how he had grabbed Evelyn at the stove. When Mom went through the front door, she looked like an artic storm had just come in. She started in on Evelyn wanting to know what she had done to entice Woody.

"Well, I never thought I would see the day that my mother would turn against me. That worthless over-sexed drunk doesn't need anyone to entice him," Evelyn said. Mom grabbed a block of coal from the bucket and threw it at her just missing her head by inches as it splattered against the wall. At this time Woody came though the kitchen door. I could see he was getting pretty drunk. Mom started in on him. Woody said if she didn't shut up he was going to slap her head off. Mom said, "Go ahead you lying coward. God knows it wouldn't be the first time." Woody went toward her then Wilma started yelling at him.

The killer instinct I didn't have earlier showed up. I remembered a fence railing that had been thrown into the woodpile earlier today. It had a long nail sticking through it. I ran out to get it and rushed toward the living room where the ruckus was still going on. Woody's back was to me. I swung the four- foot railing with all the strength I had in me, intending to sink the nail deep into his brain. There was a large archway separating the living room from the kitchen. With a loud crack the board broke. I was left with a one- foot piece in my hand, and the three - foot piece was hanging from the archway with the nail imbedded in the wall. Everyone had been screaming at each other, even the old dog was barking in the excitement. Now everything went quiet. Woody looked at the board hanging from the nail he knew was intended for him. He said, "I'm getting out of this place. You're all a bunch of crazy fools. Somebody is going to get killed." So he got his hat and coat and left. We all watched him as he disappeared down the road toward the store. We found out the next day Woody had caught the bus back to Kentucky.

For the next day or two Mom and Evelyn were cool toward each other and stayed out of each other's way. Mom had me tell what had gone on the past two days until I got tired of telling it. Then she would ask John to tell what happened and what he saw. I guess she was looking for a reason for the outburst to the girls. Things settled down after a day or two, except Mom cried a lot. She became very depressed and we were worried, but didn't know how to help her.

We got back in school and the mornings were icy cold, but very little snow. Eight or ten days after Woody left, we got off the school bus at the store. There was a letter there for Mom. When we gave her the letter, as she was reading it, we could tell she was troubled by it.

"What's wrong?" I asked.

"Oh, nothing," she said. "Woody wants me to come home."

"But you're not going to, are you Mom?" I asked.

"The county is wanting money for back taxes on the farm. If it ain't one thing it's another," she said as she raised the cover to the stove and threw the letter in the fire. The tears started flowing from Mom's eyes again and I felt the tears welling up in my own eyes. I didn't want them to see me cry so I hurried outside.

When I opened the door, our dog Bingo was curled up in a ball to keep warm. He was lying against the door. He could probably feel the warmth from inside. The tears were flowing, causing me to stumble over the dog. I took out my frustration on him. I cussed, kicked and beat on him until he ran under the porch and hid. I definitely had lots of anger in me. It was dark when I calmed down and came back into the house. Mom, Chuck, and Shirley were all huddled together on the couch with a blanket wrapped around them. The coal oil lamp was flickering, and after being outside in the cold air, it seemed so cozy and warm. We could have been taken for a normal family.

The next day, on our way home from school, about halfway there, we saw Mom coming down the road with the old tattered suitcase in her hand. There is no way to explain the hurt, the heartbreak and defeated feeling of bitterness, rejection and hopelessness when Mom told us she was going back to Kentucky. "But, only to get some business taken care of," she said.

We had been down that road too many times before to believe it would only be for a short time. It still pains me as I remember back. I can still see so clearly, Shirley, as she threw down her lunch pail and lay down on the cold frozen ground and sobbed until it wrenched our hearts out. Mom said she didn't have time to explain because she had to hurry and catch the bus to Kentucky. We watched Mom walk out of our lives and we didn't have any more contact with her until late spring.

Christmas came with snow and icy winds. It looked to be a cold winter. John and I found a good pine tree and the girls had fun making cotton balls to put on it, but we had nothing to put under the tree for gifts. We were only allowed to buy the very necessities at the store. We were out of feed for the mule. He had a hundred acres to forge in but seemed to want to hang around the barn, maybe for warmth or hoping for some grain. It turned out to be one of the coldest years anyone could remember.

January came with heavy snow that froze so hard we could walk on top of it. Ice cycles hung from the eaves of the house all the way to the ground. Schools were closed, as it was too hazardous for children to be out. February was probably the worst month for us. The coal pile was starting to get dangerously low. Once gain we spent days around the cook stove wrapped in blankets. We were undernourished and had bad colds for weeks. We probably had pneumonia. Our lungs were congested and we could hardly breathe. Evelyn probably suffered the worst. She had to cook and care for the smaller kids. Our canned goods froze and busted. They were so frozen that we could peel the glass off and the vegetables were like a solid rock. We were able to pick the glass out, but sometimes apiece would still be found while we were eating. We had no other options, either eat the food or starve. All of our food supply, including the frozen potatoes, was getting very low. We were praying for an early spring. We ran out of kindling wood and I wished I had listened to Woody and gotten in a bigger supply. John and I thought of tearing the siding off the fruit house. It was about an 8x10 building. Though it was the only dry wood available, we decided to cut down an oak tree instead. Being it was in a dormant stage, it would dry out pretty fast stacked behind the cook stove, which was going all day long. We could add it to our coal supply. Our cross cut saw hadn't been sharpened in over a year and sawing was slow hard work with the 20 degree below weather and our constant coughing when we got warmed up. It took three or four times longer to saw the frozen logs than it would have in the summer when it should have been done.

When February went, so did our food supplies. It had warmed up to about ten degrees. We were out of flour and brown beans, which we ate every day when available. We knew we had to get supplies or starve. Wilma and I went to the Mullins store. We hadn't been there since Christmas. Max, the big man that had come by with Woody was there. There were also three or four others who I had seen around, but didn't know their name. They were sitting on a wooden keg around the pot -bellied stove. They had such a hot fire going that the stovepipe was bright red. The store was only about a twenty by twenty building. We hadn't been this warm in months. Max looked at us for a long time and said he thought we had gone back to Kentucky. Orrie got two cups and poured hot chocolate in them from a pot that was sitting on a metal platform built on the side of the stove. I had never smelled or tasted anything so good. It was made with whole milk and had thick cream poured on top of it. Orrie said she thought we had gone to Kentucky for Christmas. They all kept staring at us until we got embarrassed. Wilma and I looked at each other, not wanting to tell her in front of all the men that we needed to charge more groceries. Finally Wilma asked Orrie if Mom had paid our bill so we could get more groceries. She looked worried and shook her head no. She took a charge pad out of a rack and looked through it and said the last time she had received any money was almost three months ago. We didn't want to be turned down and Wilma looked at me hoping for some kind of support but I just stood there with my hands in my pockets, staring at the floor where all the cigarette butts had been stamped out. Our hearts raced when Orrie said, "Well I may be able to let you have a few things to last you a week or two and I'll write your folks again and if I don't hear from them in two weeks, I just can't afford to extend any more credit." Wilma gave her list to Orrie. She looked at it and shook her head, but started loading up large sacks of beans, cornmeal, lard, powdered milk and twenty five pounds of flour. It was like hitting the lottery.

"You kids need to get back to school," Orrie said as we were leaving.

"We have been studying at home," Wilma said, but the only thing I had read in three months was a couple of funny books of Tarzan and Superman. It was a long walk back home, carrying about fifty pounds of food. The cold air in our lungs burned like fire, and our weakened condition made the walk hard, but our spirits were up. We would have food tonight.

Well, the first of April found us down to the last of our potatoes. The only thing left in the fruit house was the straw and broken glass that had once held our vegetables. We were down to brown beans and water gravy and very little of that. I hadn't had any shells for the gun in months but still had two traps I had borrowed from Elmer Holly and was able to catch a rabbit now and then. Bingo, the dog was staying healthier than we were. He must have been going to the other farms and getting handouts.

Spring showed up, not one day too early. We were familiar with the edible plants. There was a big variety, although some of them didn't taste too good, but the taste didn't matter too much and it didn't stop us from putting them in the cooking pot. Some of the wild greens were rock lettuce, speckle - Beckley, crows' foot, and my favorite, poke. Even dandelions were turned into a salad as soon as their little heads poked out of the ground. Crawdads were back in the creek and they were a tasty treat when found, as were birds, especially robins when we could capture them.

I doubt if there was a more starved, sickly bunch of kids in all of Virginia. I have often wished I could have had a group picture of us kids, but it would still break my heart when I would look at it.

Spring came too late for blind Jim. I found him in the upper end of the valley. He had been dead a long time. The animals had been feeding on him. That's probably why my dog was in such good shape. I felt sorry for old Jim. He had been a good mule and I hated to see his end come this way. While I was hunting for Jim, I came upon a moon -shine still. It was camouflaged so good I was within ten feet of it before I saw it. I immediately became nervous. I had heard many stories of people being killed from walking in on moon shiners. I didn't want to be one of them, so I quickly walked on by as if I hadn't seen it. My heart sank when a deep voice called out to me, "stay right there, boy." I froze in my tracks, my eyes trying desperately to find the person of the voice who spoke to me. Then Max Sturgill stepped out. I felt some relief as I knew Max, but he was holding a rifle in his hand. He asked me what I was looking for and I told him I had been looking for my mule and had found him dead. Max didn't say anything for a long time just looked at me. I almost broke down, crying as I told him he didn't have to worry about me telling anyone what I had seen. Max was still looking at me. I began thinking I had survived the winter and was still going to end up like blind Jim. I could feel the rabbit in my feet waking up and I was just getting ready to dive into the thick under brush when Max said, "I know you won't, son." My feet still wanted to go for it but the warmth in his voice stopped me. He said, "I know you won't tell anyone, son. Come on over and sit down by me." I walked over into the little ten by ten clearing where Max sat down. There was a small woodpile and I sat down on it. Then Max told me he made a deal with Woody to use the farm to set up his still because of its remoteness. While he was talking, two more men came out of the brush, both carrying shotguns. They had been with Max in the store about a month back. After awhile I got over my nervousness and Max shared his lunch with me. They were just getting things set up again. They hadn't run any whiskey since last fall. Now I knew where Woody got his whiskey.

Max and I became good friends. I enjoyed his company. They worked the still at night so no one could see the smoke. At daybreak they put the fire out, but the beer in the tubs would stay warm all day. I spent as much time with Max and the Boggs brothers as they would let me. Max treated me like a son and would give me a dollar or two now and then to buy food for the other kids. He also furnished me with twenty-two shells so I could hunt around the area where the still was and keep an eye on it. I enjoyed sitting around the still at night, listening to them tell stories. A lot of the stories were about the women in their lives. I listened very closely to these stories giving my young mind lots of things to think about.

Back in March, Orrie had written mom asking for payments on our grocery bill and had received twenty dollars with promises of more soon. It was now late April and still no mom and no money. Orrie asked John and me if we would go with her and her oldest son, Bill to Kentucky and talk with our Mom. I said we would. We were all excited about going. Her husband was working in the woods as a logger in a town called Myrtle Point, Oregon. They were talking about selling the store and moving west. This bothered me. Her kids were our best friends and the new owner may not let us charge groceries.

We rode in the back of the pickup truck and it was exciting to see the familiar places. We stopped at the watering hole. It seemed so long ago that we were there and Mom was driving the coal truck. I yelled out directions where to turn and John and I both were filled with excitement as we went past the school. When we pulled into the wide spot in front of our house, it was as if I had never left. It still looked like home, every tree and bush I had climbed and hid behind looked the same. John and me jumped out of the truck and ran up to the house. It never once dawned on me that Mom wouldn't be happy to see us. Instead of a hug and a welcoming smile, she wanted to know what we were doing there. I told her Orrie was moving and needed money. "You are going to be sorry for this, young man," she said and walked out to the truck to talk with Orrie.

Jack and Jerry came out on the porch where John and I were standing. We looked at each other. I was surprised how much they had grown since I had last seen them. They were both cotton tops with lots of hair.

"Is that you, big brother?" Jack asked me with his sparkling blue eyes.

"Yes, it's me I said.

"Are you going to stay with us?" he wanted to know.

"I don't know until I've talked to Mom." I said. About that time Mom came on the porch. She wasn't a happy camper. If looks could kill I would have died there on the porch.

"If you haven't messed me up by bringing her over here," Mom said. "You and John get yourselves back in that truck and when I get back over there, you both will wish you had never been born." If she had beaten me with a club, it wouldn't have hurt as much as the rejection. With heads down and almost in tears we went back out and climbed into the bed of the truck. Mom came back out with a check for Orrie and a dirty look for John and me. Once again with hurt and rejection, bitterness and a heavy heart, we watched as the home where we both were born and grew up in, faded in the distance.

I was depressed for days and lost interest in doing anything except spending time with Max and the guys. I was still missing more school than I went. I had gotten in a fight with a boy at school. I took a lot of frustration out on him and was brought before the principal. When the principal looked at my portfolio he started asking a lot of questions. When I didn't answer him and just sat there, he got mad and said he was going to keep an eye on me and I had better start shaping up or else. I was still mad when I got on the bus. It was a seven- mile ride to where I got off at the store. But about half way there, the boy I had gotten in the fight with earlier was looking my way and laughing. My temper rose again. I went over and punched him in the nose again. His buddy grabbed me and we had a free for all. The bus driver ran back and separated us. After asking some questions, he put me off the bus and said I couldn't ride the bus anymore. I had about four miles left to home. I got madder as I went. I had picked up a bunch of new cuss words from Max and the boys. I used them over and over and then invented a bunch more. I cussed everything and everybody, who ever thought, said, or did anything to me. I told Max what had happened. He laughed and thought it funny. He said I didn't need all that education anyhow. Max said he had only gone to the fourth grade and had survived just fine. He handed me a jar of moonshine and told me it would settle me down. I tipped the fruit jar up and took a big drink. It burned all the way down, but put a warm glow in me that I liked, and after a couple minutes I tilted the fruit jar again. It instantly gave me a warm relaxed feeling. Max said that was enough to make all my troubles go away, that I couldn't have anymore. That wasn't the first time I had tried moonshine but it was the first time I liked it.

As you can see, Max had a big influence on my life. Besides the drinking, cussing, smoking, whiskey running and womanizing, he also had a bad habit. That was cock- fighting, known as gaming roosters. There was a lot of betting and whiskey drinking. It was held in big barns around the country, always at night. There was big money won and lost. It wasn't unusual to see doctors, lawyers and law enforcement people there. Even one judge attended regularly. I didn't have any money to bet, but I liked watching the roosters fight to the death. I never thought of it as cruel or even as wrong, raising and selling gaming chickens. It was as common as pigs and cows. Most of the men felt the same way I did. It was years after I had left the mountain country before I felt differently.

One morning a car pulled up in the yard and two men got out. They had dress clothes on and looked official. We all became frightened. Evelyn went to the door and they asked if our mom or dad was home. "No," she said, but maybe she could help them. They gave their names and said they worked for the county and wanted to ask some questions. They wanted to know where our folks were. "In Kentucky." she said,

"When are you expecting them back?" they asked.

"Well," she drawled slowly, stalling for time while her mind raced for the right words. "I'm not real sure," she said. The men looked at each other and one started to write on a pad. We knew something was wrong but didn't know what. We were getting more nervous as they continued to ask how many kids were in our family, how old they were and the biggest question, how many days in a month did they go to school? All our hearts did flip-flops. "I'm not sure" Evelyn said. "They have been sick a lot." He went on to ask all of our names and our ages. She was almost in tears by now and said "The kids are feeling better now and I can promise you they will be in school every day. I can sure promise you that." They just looked at each other and smiled.

"We would like to look around inside if it's ok with you," one man said.

"Well I don't mind, but it will embarrass me to death. I haven't finished cleaning."

"Oh, don't worry about that," they said. We all gathered in a huddle and watched nervously as they went from room to room. After looking through the kitchen cupboards, they once again wrote on the note pad. "How long has it been since you've seen your folks?" the one with the pad asked.

"Quite awhile" Evelyn said.

"Can you tell me about how many days?" She glanced our way for some kind of support, but none was given.

"Well it's been a right smart while. I guess four or five months," she said. The man entered this information in the pad and stuck it in his pocket, reached over and rubbed Chuck's head. Chuck ran into the bedroom. That's what we all would like to have done. The men thanked Evelyn and got into their car and left, leaving us kids with a lot of unanswered questions.

That night when I met the guys at the still, I told them about the two men coming to our house. Max looked worried and asked a lot of questions about it and I told him all I knew. The next night when I showed up at the still site, it was all cleaned and tidy with no evidence there was ever a still there. They had even buried the ashes from the fires.

They had dug up plants from another place and planted them where the area had been trampled down. Even I could hardly tell anyone had been there.

This bothered me greatly. Max had been like a father to me and I sure didn't want to see him move the still out of the area. I felt something was going on but couldn't figure out what it was. I asked at the grocery store if they had seen Max, but no one was helpful and Orrie seemed nervous. I didn't know for months that she had talked to the government people about us kids being there by ourselves. I don't know what would have happened if someone hadn't taken a stand. Max was afraid the government men may have frightened me into saying something about the still, so he chose to be on the safe side and lay low for awhile. It was five years before I saw Max again.

CHAPTER 4

Back to Kentucky

About two weeks after the surprise visit from the government men, we got a surprise visit from Mom and Woody. The coal truck came creeping up the rough road and like the Kentucky farm, we were told to load up our stuff, we were moving back to Kentucky. Evelyn had been seeing Clyde Sturgill and he asked her to marry him. Now that we were moving back to Kentucky, she decided to stay in Virginia and marry Clyde. I never knew if it was for love or escape. Mom left a few things there for her to use.

Within a couple hours we had the truck loaded and with very mixed emotions we once again crawled on top of the furniture and started down the overgrown road that we had become so familiar with.

My life had become filled with good and bad memories. It seemed that every tree and path we passed had a story to log in my mind. I saw the mountain teaberries that we picked and ate on the way to and from school, the mulberry tree that we had stripped clean of it's delicious fruit and the sarvis tree with it's sweet red berries, the trails leading through the rhododendron bushes where John and I had set steel traps for rabbits and sometimes we would get a red fox. A good pelt would bring two dollars and fifty cents. Evelyn had left earlier with Phyllis and had walked down to Clyde's house. I suspect there were tears falling to the ground as she went. There was surely going to be a vacuum in our lives. She had gone more than the extra mile for her brothers and sisters and we would miss her greatly.

The truck stopped at the entrance of our property. There was an old wooden gate that had never been closed while we lived there. Woody and the trucker had drug it closed and hooked the old rusty wire around the gatepost and so closed another chapter of my life as a child.

There must have been great fear instilled in Mom and Woody. I never knew what all took place. I heard they almost went to jail. Things became much better. We all moved back into the home where I was born and we had a fairly normal life. Woody was working in a mine. We planted a large garden, and Woody wasn't drinking as much or was as mean as he once was. Also, John and I were pretty big boys now and we didn't run very easily anymore.

Wilma was talking marriage to Raymond Polly, a boy she went to school with. Mom was with child again. This would be the eleventh child she would give birth to. Woody and I got along good. We went on some good hunting trips together. He even shared his moonshine with me.

December of the following year of leaving Virginia, I became sixteen. The spring after my sixteenth birthday, my Uncle Vernon, mom's brother, came by for a visit. He had been living in California for the past three years and entertained us with stories of great wealth to be made in the logging industry. He claimed to be making a hundred dollars a day falling redwood trees. This was real wealth to us. The coalmines were paying twelve dollars and fifty cents for a ten-hour work- day.

As the evening wore on and the moonshine got passed around, I asked him if he thought I could get a job there. He said the saw mill was in need of workers because the draft had taken most of the young men into the service. The mills paid fifteen to eighteen dollars a day. I privately asked Mom if I could go back to California with Vernon. She hesitated only briefly and said if Vernon would take me it was ok with her, but it was going to put a big load on her and John with the extra garden work. Vernon had tilted the whiskey jar for about the fourth time when I asked him if he would take me back with him. "Well, I would like that," he said. "I would like having you out there. You could stay with me. I've got a two bedroom house and we could share the rent." I walked outside on cloud nine. It was just turning dark and the evening light was highlighting the yellow paint on the fresh waxed, brand new 1950 Mercury convertible. I've never been more excited and happy than I was that evening. To think I could be so lucky as to go cross- country in the most beautiful car I had ever seen. Yet at the same time I was scared. I knew that I had a lot to learn. My worldly knowledge only reached fifty miles, from the Kentucky farm to the Virginia farm.

The night closed in around me and the mountains looked dark and huge as they poked their tops into the starry sky. The years had made me doubt about there being a God, why He would let all the bad things happen to helpless kids, but tonight as I looked up into the starry sky, I felt a spiritual closeness that I had never known before and if indeed He was up there, I wanted to thank Him for opening this door of opportunity. I prayed for Him to watch over my family and protect Mom through the childbirth. I prayed her and Woody would get along with each other and that they would keep the family together.

Tears started running down my face when I thought of not being able to be with my brother John. We were so close. We could always tell each other about our hopes and dreams as well as our fears. Everybody needs someone they can trust enough to tell all their secrets to. As bad as I was going to miss John, I knew I had to take this opportunity and I would be in that yellow convertible heading west in the morning.

CHAPTER 5

California, Here I Come

I didn't get very much sleep that night; I was so excited about the trip to California. My mind kept dragging me through Hollywood and the other great places. I was a movie star riding along side of Tex Ritter, Tom Mix or one of the other great cowboys. It seems like my eyes had hardly closed when Mom shook me awake. "It's time to get up and eat. Vernon wants to get an early start." I put on my best clothes for traveling, went out on the porch and threw cold water from the aluminum wash pan onto my swollen eyes. I felt tired and scared and would have liked to put off leaving one more day. All of a sudden I became frightened of leaving my family and the things that I was a part of, the mountains that I had hunted in and run to for protection. What if I didn't like California? What if I couldn't handle the sawmill work? "Fred quit your daydreaming and get ready," Mom yelled at me. I wanted to tell her I had changed my mind, but the words wouldn't come out. I sat down at the table where most everyone was through eating. Vernon and Woody looked like I felt, tired and sleepy. There wasn't any laughing or excitement in them this morning. The moonshine had left them with a big hangover,

Mom had put two pairs of pants and two shirts in a paper bag along with three pair of socks and a black pocket comb. That was my total possessions, no shorts, hanky or extra shoes. Mom gave me twenty dollars, plus a lot of advice like what to do and what not to do, such as "don't let your Uncle Vernon take your money and when you get to work be sure and send money home so I can save it for you." That reminded me of the summer I worked in the coal mine. Two dollars for a miners' hat and the rest she was saving for me. I promised her I would send what I could. Vernon said, "Freddie boy, are you ready to head west?" "I'm ready if you are." I told him, picking up my sack of clothes and starting for the car, having no idea what road we would take to go west.

I wanted to hug everyone and say I love you, but I felt too embarrassed to do so. No one spoke for a while then Shirley said, "Bye brother." Mom told Vernon to take good care of her boy. I looked for John, but he had disappeared. My heart felt heavy and I could hardly hold back the tears as we drove out from the old home place and once again I felt fear climbing up into my throat. Even though my uncle was right beside me, I felt scared and alone.

Vernon asked me where the best place to buy moonshine was. I told him where Woody bought his. Vernon came out of the Coalminer's Inn with two pints of moonshine. "I need a taste of the hair of that dog that bit me," Vernon said. I would hear those words many times in the future. I never saw the Coalminer's Inn again. It later burned down, but I'm sure there were others to take its place.

Uncle Vernon was a handsome man, six feet, muscular with gray hair, and a dark mustache. His number one goal in life was to chase the ladies and he managed to catch a few. Young or old didn't deter him from his goal. Though I didn't know what an alcoholic was at that time, I learned

Vernon was one. Though he was still in his middle thirties, he consumed a fifth of whiskey daily, but he could still function fairly good. His boldness quite often got him into trouble. He was a pretty good fighter and got the chance to practice quite often when trying to seduce married women. Sometimes the husbands would take him outside for a little walk to teach him some respect and more times than not he would be the first one back in. I could always tell how the fight went. He had a cocky bounce to his walk and a smile with his gold tooth shining when he won. I would learn a lot of bad habits from Vernon over the next few years.

The excitement of traveling finally pushed out the fear and after a few hours, we were out of the mountains. The lush green grass for miles blew my mind. In the hill country, a twenty-acre meadow was big and a forty acre one was huge. Here mile after mile of ranch and farmland flew by. Beautiful plantation homes sat off in the distance. They were big and impressive. I told Vernon that I never knew there were homes that big. "They are prestige homes" he said. I thought about that, not knowing what "Prestige" meant. I figured it must be the name of the people that built it. So when I saw those white fences and huge homes, I said, "Those prestige builders sure get around. They have built most of the houses for the last fifty miles. Vernon laughed and said, "I can see that I've got a lot of work to do with you, Freddie boy." My face got red as Vernon explained what "prestige" meant.

I think that was the first time I realized my need for a better education. I now had to apply myself to learning and I also knew that someday I wanted to be wealthy enough to have one of those prestige homes. I had seen enough poverty to last me a lifetime.

Vernon knew a lot of people. I was impressed as we rolled into Pocatello, Idaho and stayed with a friend of his, who was a bank manager. It was a fun stop, warm and friendly people who made sure we were well cared for. I was at my most awkward stage and it seemed I couldn't walk through the house without knocking something over. I had never sat at a table so fancy and had no idea what fork to use. I didn't even know what kind of food I was eating, but no one seemed to notice when I messed up. Later Vernon clued me in on some of the things I did wrong or things I should have done, but didn't.

I got very excited when Jack, our host said he wanted to take us fishing in the morning. Jack had the privilege of fishing a stream that went through miles of private property. Sunrise found us on the bank of a slow- moving stream, fishing for what was supposed to have trophy size rainbow trout and lots of them. Jack and Vernon pulled out three fancy fishing rods. I had never seen a fly rod before and had not the slightest idea how to use it. Vernon said, "Just watch and you will catch on real easy." All that casting didn't make much sense to me. I was a cane pole fisherman with lots of patience. I would sit on the riverbank for hours dangling a worm on a homemade hook, waiting for a fish with a low IQ to come by. I never heard of catch and release. If it was large enough to get my hook into its mouth, it would end its days in a frying pan. Now Jack and Vernon were telling me they had to be over twelve inches long to keep. Jack handed me a metal telescopic rod with a reel on it. I didn't have the slightest idea how to use it so I sat down and watched them make a bunch of false casts. They let this little imitation fly made with feathers and horsehair land on the water, then pull it back in and do the same thing over and over again. It looked like more work than fun. Jack said we would release all the fish we caught for the next couple hours, but were allowed to keep two fish per person over twelve inches. He said just to keep the ones that were fifteen inches and over. I had my fly line just about everywhere but in the water. Lucky there weren't any tall trees around but none of the bushes escaped my casting. Swatting was more like what

I was doing. No sensible fish would have stayed within a hundred feet of me.

Jack and Vernon were having lots of fun. They were catching fish on the horse- hair and feathers and were yelling with excitement. This made me eager to get my fly line to cast properly instead of my waving the fly rod like I was conducting a rock and roll band.

I sat down disgusted with myself. Then I realized there were lots of grasshoppers buzzing around. I quickly got into Jack's tackle box and took off the horsehair fly and replaced it with a medium size plain hook. I then chased down the grasshoppers and soon had one pinned on my hook. I peeled off some line from the reel, picked it up and literally threw it out into the water, and just sat down and watched as the line slowly drifted down stream. I had hardly gotten comfortable, when the biggest rainbow I had ever seen exploded out of the water. It hung in the air long enough for my mind to record a picture that has lasted a lifetime. I knew nothing of using the drag on the reel to let the fish tire itself down. Instead I did what I had always done before. I grabbed the line and snubbed the fish, causing it to perform its acrobatic jump once more, parting my hook and hopper. This happened four more times that morning. I didn't land one fish, but it was probably the most exciting and fun day I had ever spent fishing. Things of high excitement as well as things of great fear have a way of remaining in one's mind for a lifetime. Hopefully, the days of pleasure far exceed the days filled with fear.

A couple days later we rolled into Orick, California, a little logging town that would be my homeport for the next couple of years. It sits a couple miles from the ocean and the average daily temperature ranges about sixty five to seventy degrees. Vernon had rented a nice two- bedroom house and this was the first time that I had ever had my own bedroom. Vernon laid down the house rules. I had to keep my room clean and my bed was to be made every day. I was to do the dishes he was to do the cooking. We would share the cost of rent and the groceries. We got there on a Friday and he said Monday we would go to the saw mills and find me a job.

Everything was new and exciting especially the huge redwood trees that were up to twenty feet through and three hundred feet tall, big diesel trucks constantly going to the mills with huge one log loads. But with all the new and exciting things going on in my life, I had a problem. I couldn't stay awake. Whether it was the coastal air or the low altitude, I don't know. In Kentucky I was up early, no problem, but here I could hardly keep my eyes open. This caused me to get fired from my first job.

I went to work right away pulling lumber on a green chain in a mill about one mile from town. The foreman took a liking to me even though I was young and inexperienced. I put in a good day's work and was more than glad when the whistle blew. The foreman came over and said he was impressed with how quick I had caught on and if I would stay with the company, he would be moving me to different positions right along and in a year or two I could work up to one of the higher paying jobs. But it didn't work out that way, because of my not being able to get out of bed. Week after week I would show up late, every two or three days. Vernon would wake me up before he left for work, but quite often I would go right back to sleep. After about two months of this, the foreman met me one morning when I came to work, hurrying in late. "Son" he said, "you are a real good worker when you are here, but I'm the foreman and I'm getting tired of doing your job while you are home snoring. So you go by the office and they will have your check ready for you." That was a long mile back home. I beat myself up ever step of the way. It's a wonder I didn't become a cripple.

I was dreading the thought of telling Vernon I had gotten fired, showing my immaturity. I thought about cashing my check and going back to Kentucky. Though I often became homesick to see my family, I knew that wasn't what I wanted to do, so I made a vow to myself to get up on time, even if I had to hook an electric shocker to my bed.

To my surprise Vernon re-acted just the opposite of what I was expecting. When I told him what had happened, he just gave that little chuckle, which came from his belly and said "well Freddie boy, I may just have to make a logger out of you. I'll talk to my boss, Youlman down at the tavern tonight and see if he needs a choker setter. If you are old enough to be a logger, you are old enough to drink a beer." So he popped the lid off a couple beers and later that evening we went down to the tavern. I climbed up on a bar stool with Vernon and Youlman. Vernon ordered three beers. I went on to be a logger doing a variety of jobs including using dynamite to blow holes under those giant redwood logs.

That evening also started another activity, sitting on the bar stool, drinking. One year later, I was just one of the boys, stopping off after work and having a beer, usually only one, but sometimes two. Weekends became party time. I really didn't know any of the loggers that didn't drink, at least on weekends. I had now graduated up to mixed drinks, rum and coke being my favorite, but also Vodka Collins. Vernon was still hitting on all the women and most every weekend, he ended up in a fight. The husbands that hated Vernon were growing by the dozens and quite often two or three men would tear into him. I had now grown into a fairly muscular young man and I would help Vernon by taking on one of the men. Unlike Vernon, I couldn't brag too much later because I was taking more lumps than I was giving.

But that changed as the months went by. The hard work I was doing put long hard muscles on my now six- foot frame. I was having more bar room fights now even when Vernon wasn't there, I should have recognized that I had a problem, but closed my eyes to it. I hated drunks, even though I was quite often one of them. It seems when people get drunk, they want to put their arms around you and when they did this to me, they would instantly find themselves on the floor with a bloody nose. There was a lot of hate and violence that rose up in me that I just couldn't seem to control. This became a way of life for me for the next few years.

I won't go into my love life out of respect for my wife. I had many relationships for the next three years. Some weren't the kind of girls you would take home to mama. Many were very quality young women, but I just couldn't trust anyone enough to be close enough to for a long-term relationship.

I was now making from twenty five to seventy five dollars per day and had managed to save a few hundred dollars. I was working with Vernon and his partner and I was involved in cutting down those giant redwoods. It was December and the winter rains had come and shut down the logging camp. Their roads weren't rocked, which was a big cost to them. They laid off most of the workers for about three months and lots of men found jobs in the saw mills that kept on working. Vernon and I didn't hire out to the mills as we had made enough money through the summer to get by the winter.

Vernon had an ex-wife and a daughter who lived in Raymond, Washington and also two uncles by the name of Henry and Hugh Standifer. I had heard Mom talk of them. She hadn't seen them since she was a young girl. Vernon decided to go see his daughter and wanted me to go with him and I agreed. Soon we were packed and on our way to Washington State. The coastal highway was curvy and was slow driving. Vernon thought he was the best driver in the whole world, especially when he had a few drinks in him. We had left about three p.m. and Vernon figured we could drive all night and be there before noon the next day. Vernon was making good time, squealing tires around every corner. Dark came and he had been hitting the bottle more than normal. I asked him about this and he said it kept him from getting tired and sleepy. About nine p.m., we hit this one corner doing about sixty mph. I knew we were in big trouble. Tires squealed and rubber peeled. We were about eighty percent around the corner when the car started sliding sideways and finally came to a stop with both back wheels hanging over a cliff. On my side of the car, I looked straight down at the ocean, over one hundred feet below. It was very close to going over so we unsnapped the convertible top and crawled over the windshield. We were both shaking in our boots. This was a worse experience than Mom with the coal truck. We were extra lucky that night. A farmer about a quarter mile down the road had a brand new John Deere tractor and agreed to pull us out for a price. We were glad to cough up the money. He hooked a big chain onto the car and literally slid it on its frame until the back tires found mother earth. Vernon paid the farmer then reached under the seat and pulled out his half bottle of whiskey and offered a drink to the farmer. "If I had known that it was the booze that got you in there, I would have left you there," he said, then climbed on his tractor and rode off into the night. Vernon gave that little chuckle tilted the bottle and took a big drink and handed me the bottle. I needed it more than him so I took the bottle and took a long swallow. Vernon's foot got a little lighter for the rest of the trip. He always blamed the highway department for improper marking. He said the reason he slid off the road was because it should have been a 15mph sign instead of a thirty mph sign.

We were both very tired and sleepy when we got to Uncle Henry and Aunt Maggie's. They were both very warm and friendly and welcomed us with open arms. They loved Vernon a lot and were eager to hear how things were going in his life. Vernon called his ex-wife and asked if she would bring his daughter Peggy over so he could visit with her. Stella said she would, but it would be a couple of hours. Aunt Maggie showed us where we would sleep. I laid down on the nice soft bed and immediately fell asleep. When I woke up, Stella and Peggy were there. They were both very beautiful people. Stella had married Vernon when she was seventeen years old and she still looked very young. As the day wore on, I felt myself growing very close to Maggie and Henry. Their life style was so different than what Vernon and I had chosen. They always prayed before each meal and Henry was very bold in telling what the Lord was doing in their lives. I wasn't too big on this religion stuff, but it did cause me to reflect back a few hours when I was looking one hundred feet down at the rocks and surf, knowing that one foot more, the car would have gone over that cliff.

It was time once again to head down the coast highway. Vernon had spent most of his time in the honkytonks, drinking and dancing with old flames. I had spent my time visiting with the Standifers. Aunt Maggie was a good cook and she kept bringing out cakes and pies and I always seemed to have room for one more slice. They begged me to stay with them and felt I could find a job there. They would rent the upstairs bedroom to me and I could eat with them.

Henry had been telling me how good the hunting and fishing was around there and he needed a good hunting partner. I was tempted, but told him I had better go back.

CHAPTER 6

Home for Christmas

As we headed back to California, I started getting home-sick to see Mom and my family. It would be Christmas in a couple weeks and also my eighteenth birthday. By the time we got back to Orick, Calif. I had made up my mind that I was going to fly back home for Christmas. Vernon tried to talk me out of it right up to the day of my flight.

It still amazes me how the human mind can flip from love, hate and bitterness and back to love. I probably should refer to it as being temporarily brain dead. I have no way of explaining how the bad times didn't seem so bad anymore and the hungry times didn't seem so real. I just knew I missed my family and I had a new baby sister, Ginny that I had never seen. I hadn't written to Mom since John had enlisted in the Paratroops. So I wrote, "I'll be home for Christmas" on a post-card and dropped it in the post office a week before my flight out of San Francisco.

I enjoyed the plane trip. It was fun because it was my first time to fly. The plane was half full of soldiers going home for Christmas.

I had forgotten how cold and icy things could get in Kentucky. It was in the upper twenties when my plane landed at the Lexington airport. I still had about a five- hour trip by bus. Finally the bus pulled into the town of Whitesburg. There wasn't any change in anything as far as I could see. As we passed the courthouse, my mind flashed back to the times I had stood in line with Mom to get our sack of food and how eager we were to start sampling the cheese and dried fruit. My mind was quickly brought back to the present as the bus came to a stop. I stepped out of the bus and looked up the hill at the Whitesburg High School. It stood out like a beacon. Some of my friends had graduated from there and others, like me had dropped out or never went at all.

I didn't have a diploma, but I had made it a number one priority in my life, to learn and I spent many hours reading and teaching myself. I wasn't the shy and dependant young boy that had left here a couple years before. There is a popular TV show called Extreme Makeover. That's how I felt. I had a long way to go, but was now self-confident that I could be anything I set my mind to. Success mostly takes lots of perseverance. One thing I didn't want was to be poor. There were three taxis sitting in front of the drugstore where one could buy a bus ticket, also hot dogs, hamburgers, soda and ice cream.

I asked one of the cabbies what the cost was to take me the other seven miles. I think it was fifty cents. He took my suitcase and loaded it into the trunk. We headed for Bottom Fork and the last leg of my journey. The cabbie said his name was Collins and when I told him my name, he said he knew my father very well. He said he was the finest man he had ever met. I heard this many times as the weeks went on, all the good things my Dad was about and it started me thinking about my life and the direction I was heading. It seemed to be totally opposite of the life style my Dad had lived.

The old school house where I had hung out looked lonely with patches of snow and ice scattered through the play yard.

I was both happy and nervous when we pulled up in front of the house. It was now late evening and lights were shining in side the house but no one came to the door to meet me. I paid Collins for the ride, got my suitcase and headed for the house when the door flew open and Mom came running out yelling "thank you Jesus, thank you Jesus, my boy is home." She threw her arms around me, squeezing the breath out of me. She stepped back and said, "Let me look at you." Tears came to both of our eyes as she said, "I wondered if I would ever see my boy again."

I was feeling awkward and was glad when Woody and all the kids came out on the porch. What got my eye first, was this beautiful baby girl with big, bright blue eyes and white platinum hair, This turned out to be my baby sister, Ginny, whom I had never seen. All the kids had grown a lot and Shirley, who was now a young woman said, "You sure have growed up brother." The boys had grown a lot, Jack more than Chuck and Jerry. Chuck's face still showed some scars from an accident he had. He had been riding his tricycle in front of the fireplace, when it tipped over and he was thrown into the fire. He had lost all of his hair and most of the skin on his face, arms and chest.

"Well, come on in," Woody said. "Norma is just about to put supper on the table. We just got your letter yesterday. Your mom said she didn't know when you would get here." There was a Christmas tree in the corner all lit up and presents scattered underneath. It brought real warmth to the house and what was better yet, was the warmth it brought to me. I can only explain it by saying my spirit was excited and full of joy. It felt so good to be back with my family.

Wilma had gotten married to Ray Polly. He was the brother of the girl she had been staying with quite a bit. They had only been married two months when he got drafted into the army. They had rented a small house about half a mile down the road from our house. I was later told that after Ray went into the service, Woody had come by her house one night, drunk. When she wouldn't let him in, he tried to force the door open. Wilma had a thirty eight special pistol and she told him if he didn't leave she was going to shoot him, so he yelled for her to go ahead and shoot. She fired over his head, through the door. Cussing, Woody said, "Shoot again!" So she shot again through the middle of the door. The bullet hit him in the side. Luckily for both of them it went through his side without hitting any vital organs, but it hurt enough to take the sex drive out of him.

After Christmas, I had to make a decision whether to go back to California or get a job. It was so nice to have all the family together again. Woody had a good job making twelve dollars a day which was good pay for that area. I found a job working for a man that was starting a brand new mine, but would only pay nine dollars a day. This was hard for me, especially after making big money in California. I worked there a few months.

Ray, Wilma's husband got discharged from the army and went to work for the same man I was working for. It was probably about April, and we had stopped loading coal inside the mine and had walked outside for a sandwich, when there was a terrible loud noise coming from inside the mine. We went in to see what had happened and found the whole mountain had fallen in. Thousands of pounds of rock had crushed the cars we had been loading. If we hadn't stopped for a sandwich, we would have been crushed along with the coal cars. I felt as if the Lord was trying to tell me something and I was going to listen, so I picked up my lunch pail and walked away from the coalmines forever.

There wasn't any work to be found and if there was anything, the soldiers coming home from the service were going to get them. I had been hearing lots of talk about good money to be made working for the big automobile companies in Detroit, Michigan. I decided to give it a try since it was only a day's drive away and I could come home three or four times a year. If you remember, Evelyn and Clyde had moved to Detroit after they got married and I was eager to see her again. It was hard to leave my brothers and sisters again.

Ginny, whom I had only known for a few months, with her blue eyes and happy smile, had stolen my heart. The young boys were lining up to court Shirley and as Tennessee Ernie Ford would say, "Was as cute as a speckled pup layin' under a brand new red wagon."

I was happy when I got to Detroit and found Evelyn and Clyde had a room I could rent. I went to work right away for a trucking firm loading and unloading semis. The pay was good and I worked nights, which gave Evelyn and Clyde their private time.

Then summer came. The days hit one hundred degrees and more with humidity ninety percent and no air conditioner in the house. Before the summer was over I went from one hundred eighty five pounds down to one hundred sixty five pounds. The union went on strike and I took a few days to drive down to Kentucky to visit my family. Clay Adams, who lived a few miles from my Kentucky home, rode down with me and I told him about my time out west.

I had been home a couple days when Clay and his father-in-law, Jim came to see me. Clay's father-in-law had been offered a job in Puyallup, Washington as the Postmaster and wanted to know if I had been there or knew anything about the town. I told him I liked Washington a lot and we all got kind of excited about it. He was a diabetic and was afraid of making the trip by him self and asked if he could hire me to drive him out there. Without much thought, I said I would. He then informed me he had to be on the job the following Monday. That left only five days to get there.

When one is young and free, it doesn't take long to pack. Early the next morning, I once again said my goodbyes to all my family. I was standing outside with mixed feelings about the decision I had made, when Jim came driving up. "Are you ready to hit the road?" he asked.

"Ready as I'll ever be," I said and crawled in behind the wheel. Jim's Buick was only about six months old and we would be almost welded to each other for the next four days. I turned to look back and said "goodbye" once again to the home where I was born, never to see it again. It burned down a few years later as did the house on the hill.

It was a long hard drive to Washington State. Jim's wife had fried a couple chickens and had sent a large thermos of coffee. I drove nonstop except for fueling up and going to the bathroom. We pulled into Puyallup with a day to spare.

Jim and I said our good byes and I caught a bus the sixty or seventy miles to Raymond where my Great Uncle Henry and Aunt Maggie lived. I found their name in a phone book and gave them a call to see if that room was still available and if it hadn't been, I was thinking about going on to California. "Yes, we have a room for you" was the reply and they said for me to get California out of my mind, they would be there to pick me up in fifteen minutes.

When I got settled in my upstairs room at the Standifers, I got a letter off to Evelyn in Detroit, Michigan. I knew she would be worried about me. She still felt like she needed to mother me. But then she had given four years of her life to mothering and caring for us kids.

Poor Evelyn, if she could have seen what disappointments, the heartbreaks, the suffering and pain she was going to go through the next thirty years, she probably would have ended it way back then, but It's God's grace and mercy we can't see the future.

I too had to go through some painful and frightening experiences that totally changed my life. But first I have to bring all my family out to Washington State. As a popular newscaster would say, "please stay tuned for the rest of the story."

CHAPTER 7

My Wife to Be

I was living with the Standifers when I met this beautiful, brown-eyed dark haired girl by the name of Marilyn Bentley, but most people call her "Lynn." I now call her my wife. It took only about three months of dating to know we loved each other and wanted to spend our lives together. I was now twenty and Lynn was sixteen and with her parents permission we got married. One week ago, even as I write this book, we celebrated fifty years of marriage, and still in love I might add.

I liked Washington and I especially liked the hunting and fishing but I kept thinking of those big redwoods and even at twenty years old, I wanted prosperity in my life and was willing to work hard for it. So one September morning found us with everything we owned in the back seat and trunk of my 1949 Ford heading to California. We couldn't have been happier. One arm on the steering wheel and the other wrapped around my wife and the radio turned up, how good can it get?

Our first daughter, Connie and our second child, Rick was born while we lived in Orick, California. We spent a couple of years having fun with our new family and bonding with each other.

I had gone back to working in the giant redwoods and getting paid by the amount of work I got done. I had many one hundred dollar days. This was three times more than the mill workers were making. Even though everything was going good in our life, I still felt an empty place within, like something was missing. I thought maybe it was my family. Mom, Woody and the kids had moved from the Kentucky farm to a house in Franklin, Ohio. We had just bought a 1953 Ford Victoria hard top convertible, and I had a week's vacation coming, so I felt this would be a good chance to go and see my family and let them meet my wife, Lynn.

We drove long hours and like so many vacations, we were very tired and sleepy when we pulled into the driveway. Mom took a liking to Lynn right away, so we had a good three -day visit.

Sister Wilma had been in a T.B. sanitarium in a town not very far away, so we were able to visit with her, also. Mom seemed very happy living in Ohio. She was working for a packinghouse butchering chickens. Woody had also found a job he liked and some of his family lived close by.

Woody had bought a Studebaker car and had learned to drive (sort of). He took me for a ride to show it off and just "happened" to go by the Keg, a neighborhood tavern. Woody wanted to stop in and he ordered jumbo pitchers for us. About a half hour later, if there had been any doubt about my intelligence, I proved it by climbing back into the Studebaker with Woody behind the wheel. Well, we did get home ok and the next morning, after a big hardy breakfast and hugs from everybody, for the third time in my life, I was again heading west.

I ended up taking another week off from work and our bank account was dragging bottom by the time I got back to work.

It was now August and it was rare to work past the end of October before the winter shut us down, thus giving me only three months to make enough money to last through the winter. I had managed to make a few extra dollars making grape stakes after the layoff. These are two inch by two inch stakes made from redwood and used to hold up grape vines. They are six feet tall.

April brought sunshine and I had been back to work a week when a telegram from Woody informed us that Mom had died suddenly. My reaction to this news was to get angry and I threw my lunch box against the wall busting my thermos. This frightened the children and they started crying. I swore to kill Woody for I felt he was somehow responsible for her death.

Not having a phone in our rented house, which was in the country, I drove to a phone booth and called my sisters. They informed me that Mom had died from a heart attack. The next morning, I knew there was a big decision that had to be made. I had only one week's pay coming and all our bills were due. My wife and kids had to be cared for and I remembered back to when I was just a small kid. A young man that respected my father had come by to ask for advice. He wanted to enlist in the army, but had doubts of what to do. "Son," my dad said, "when you become a man, there will be important decisions that will have to be made. The decisions you make will be with you for the rest of your life. So try to make the very best one you can and hope it doesn't come back to haunt you." The young man went on to make a career in the army and lived happily ever after.

Right now I wasn't very happy. I was feeling sorry for my mother. I thought back to all the hardships she had gone through in her short 47 years. She had given birth to eleven children, many of those days before washing machines, automatic clothes dryers and electric stoves. Cooking, cleaning, putting herself last, she had never known anything but hard work and caring for babies.

Though I was still bitter for the way she treated us, I could see how free she must have felt when Woody came by with his relaxed, "don't worry" attitude. I found a quiet place, sat down and let the tears flow as I remembered the good and the bad, and then I buried my mother, choosing to remember her the way I saw her seven months before. Not going to her funeral has come back to haunt me a few times, but I have learned to make the very best decision I can at the time, then go on with life.

The fall of 1958, the year my Mom died, was another short season for work. We had just gotten a couple thousand dollars ahead, and then got laid off. I stopped in at the Lumberjack Tavern and washed down my sorrows with a couple beers. A couple guys I knew said they were getting ready to go to Mexico for the winter. "You can take a thousand dollars down there and live like a king" he said. The exchange was twenty to one. I started thinking that I was in the wrong trade when one had to move to Mexico for half the year.

Instead of south, we decided on going north, back to Washington, close to Lynn's folks, which she hardly ever got to see. I was working in an oyster cannery when we got married and they told me if I should come back to Washington I would have a job with them. We came to California with a trunk load of goods, now we were heading back to Washington with a U-Haul trailer.

We rented a house with five acres of land. Connie and Rick loved this and so did Lynn and I. I immediately went to work for the oyster company. We weren't living like kings, but had access to the finest oysters, clams, ling- cod and shrimp on the west coast.

My youngest brother Chuck came out to Washington and lived with us for a while. He was eighteen and worked as a logger for a while, then moved to Myrtle Point, Oregon where Vernon was. He then went to work in a plywood plant. He married Joanne and they had two kids, Charmia and Gabe. A couple of years later they moved back to Washington where they had another baby boy. He died from meningitis. They divorced shortly after that.

Brother John was next to move to Washington. He and his wife Opal had been living on the farm in Virginia. They didn't do too well at farming, but were great at making kids. They had four kids in four years; Norma Jean, Keta, Rocky and Barbara. They stayed with us a few days until they found a house that was big enough, yet was affordable.

I got John a job at the oyster plant, but he had the weakest stomach of anyone I ever knew. Most people got used to the smell of the oysters and shrimp in a couple of days, but not John. He worked there three days and there wasn't an hour went by that he wasn't gagging and throwing up. He hadn't been able to eat and nothing was left to throw up. I was concerned for him because he was so pale. But by noon on the third day John felt he wouldn't ever be able to handle the smells and quit the oyster business.

We lived in a small town and there weren't a lot of jobs that somehow didn't involve fishing and logging or sawmill work. John didn't like any of the above. But after a couple of months he took a job working in a tire recap shop. It only paid minimum wage, which was a dollar twenty five cents and hour, but at least it didn't smell like fish. Opal went to work waiting tables for the same minimum wage, plus tips. They were poor but happy.

For a long time I had been wanting my own business, but like most young people raising a family, it was hard to stay even, let alone getting enough money ahead to start a business. Lynn's sister and brother-in-law had moved to Ft. Bragg California a year earlier. He was falling timber for this company and had closed the season averaging one hundred twenty five dollars a day. They were figuring on starting back up in a few days, about April 1, and were going to need one more cutter.

Well, without following my dad's advice or thinking it through, about three days later we were headed south on Interstate 5 in a Ford station wagon, towing a U-Haul trailer, with visions of big dollar signs and starting my own logging company. But it didn't turn out that way. Instead it turned out to be the wettest spring in the past few years. April came and went. It continued to rain and still no work. May came and no work. I finally took a job for a sawmill forty miles away.

The only good thing I can remember about that year was our daughter Debbie was born at Ft Bragg hospital on June 26, 1961. We gave it one more year and the same old story, big money for a few months and then no work. We said our final goodbyes to California as a place to work. Rolling stones don't gather any moss, but they don't gather any money, either. So we ended up once again in Raymond, Washington.

John was still at the same tire shop and was doing the recapping for the logging and dump truck tires and was now making two dollars and fifty cents an hour and was still happy. In a few years John became manager for a large tire company.

Wilma was next to come and join us with her husband Raymond. She also brought Jack and little sister Ginny. Wilma had gone to beauty school in Kentucky and she went to work right away and Ray went to work in a shake mill. Wilma was never able to have children, so Jack and Ginny lived with her and Ray.

Wilma was very aggressive and a hard worker. The famous coastal town of Westport, Washington was about forty miles from Raymond. It was a popular sport fishing and recreational town. Wilma opened a beauty shop there in a room of a small motel. About a year later she bought a motel and moved her shop there. About that time her and Ray weren't getting along and they finally divorced. She had a lease with option to buy an older farmhouse with three acres. She was moving to Westport and was going to let the lease on the farm go. It was in need of some repairs but had good possibilities.

I was now self-employed cutting right of way for logging roads for Weyerhaeuser and Boise Cascade. This house would be a good location for us and we talked to the owners and made a deal. Soon we were moved in. It took about a year to remodel and add a double garage to it, but it made a great first home.

Shirley and her husband Dillard, or Red as he was usually called, were next to come. They had five children; Ron, Debbie, Steve, Sandra and Johnnie Ray. Tony would be born later. Brother Jerry came out with them as he had been living in Ohio with Woody.

I remember the picnic we had at our little mini farm. It looked like a kid farm. There were about thirteen or fourteen of them, all combined and we had one more on the way. Our third daughter Judy was born on August 4, 1964. We felt four was enough, so I paid my Dr. a visit.

Red liked to hunt and fish, so we spent quite a few days doing that and we even managed to take a couple elk and deer. Shirley and Lynn were content being mothers. They spent lots of time together at the ball fields, parks and swimming holes. Sometimes Opal and her four kids would join them and when the doors opened it looked like recess at an elementary school. Those were good profitable years for Woolworth in their diaper department.

Good times come and go, it seems. That's the case with my families' wives and husbands. Shirley and Red started having marital problems and after a couple years in Washington, they divorced. Red stayed in the area for a while, and later went back to Ohio to his old job with General Motors. At this time, Jerry, who had been living with them, went to Westport to live with Wilma, who was now married to Dan, a deputy sheriff.

She was involved in a remodeling job on her motel, and with Wilma, no one was exempt from work, husband or kids. The same work habits that seemed to be running through most of my family, was definitely in Wilma. She soon opened up a wig shop in the town of Aberdeen, population of about twenty thousand and also started selling pottery and pictures from Mexico. She bought a nice two- story home on the beach with a forever ocean view.

CHAPTER 8

Kodiak, Alaska

The companies that I had been working for built roads five or more years ahead and we had this much built ahead. Jobs were getting farther apart and I did some hourly work, but I liked being my own boss.

The cannery that I had last worked for asked me if I would go to Kodiak, Alaska as manager of one of their shrimp plants and offered me a generous salary. I agreed to go for three months to check it out before moving my family.

So for the first time in our married life, I kissed my wife goodbye and left her in charge of our family. John and Shirley both lived close by and I felt they would be there quickly if Lynn had any problems.

When I landed in Kodiak, it was only a few months after the big earthquake in 1964 that devastated Alaska. A tidal wave had hit Kodiak and wiped out most of all the businesses and homes that had ocean frontage. This included the airport. I now understood the high salary.

They had about a size twenty by twenty plywood building that had been quickly erected. This contained an oil furnace

121

and a couple counter tops made from plywood. That was the airport.

The plant superintendent met me and took me to the apartment the company had rented for me. The roads were worse than most logging roads. They were covered with crushed volcanic rock and the dust was terrible.

We put my gear away and went to take a look at the cannery that would almost be my home for the next two years. They were still rebuilding the inside of the cannery. The superintendent said, "You probably need a drink after seeing all this work to be done."

"Yep," I said, "I think that would be appropriate."

"We'll stop by Solley's," he said. Now Solley's had been a big nightclub that had gotten destroyed in the tidal wave. There had been about half a dozen, but it was the only one that had been built back. The biggest businesses in town, besides the canneries, were the nightclubs. They liked being close to the waterfront, convenient to their biggest clients, the fishermen. That was the first of many trips I would make to Solley's.

I had some knowledge of welding and electrical work. In about a month we had new flumes, motors and peeler machines installed. The peeler machines were what removed the shell from the shrimp. It was a big day when we got a crew of about one hundred people. I kicked on the switch and most everything worked. What didn't was minor and was soon fixed. It took awhile to move the people around to where I felt they were best suited and in a couple months had the production back to as high as it had ever been. The work was very interesting and I got along great with most of the crew.

There were some upper level employees that left but there won't be a name or why. It would be unfair to them. The company was happy with the way I was doing things and offered a bonus of so much per case and would ship my family up plus rent us a house. I accepted their offer and soon had my wife and kids with me. My daughter Judy took her first solo steps in Alaska.

If I had chosen a time in life to live, the1800's when the west was settled, would have been the time. I could have been a fur trapper for beaver or a meat hunter for the railroad, a guide for the pioneers, etc. But my wife and girls hated Kodiak. I don't know if there ever was a park in town, but at this time there wasn't even a swing set for the kids. This was as close as one could get without going back to early America. There were thousand pound brown bear only a mile out of town, also elk, deer and caribou close by.

Lynn had never been a complainer, but was giving out some pretty big hints that she wasn't planning on making Kodiak a long- term home. I kept promising her as soon as we got a good bank account built up we would go back to Washington where we had our home rented out.

We had now been there close to a year. My company had rented another cannery and was building a brand new one. I had hand picked crews in both plants and we were now doubling our production. That meant my bonus had also doubled and was bumping my salary. I had chosen some very good foremen to oversee the crew. This gave me a little more freedom, though I was still working sixteen hours a day. I still managed to stop at Solley's as a regular and I still had my hot temper and would occasionally get into a brawl.

The owner of the company came up from Seattle and was looking into the possibility of running the plants twenty -four hours a day. I encouraged this and soon had two twelve-hour a day shifts going in both plants. We soon became one of the world's largest shrimp producers. This was a big feather in my hat.

Well, things came to a head one night when I took Lynn out to dinner to the grand opening of Solley's new nightclub. We had a nice lobster tail dinner and were having a few after dinner drinks when a couple guys I knew came over and sat down at our table. They owned a crab fishing boat. I didn't like the way one of the guys was coming on to my wife so I punched him out. His partner didn't like that, so we went at it. He went down and out. Most of the people in there didn't know what had happened, but they were ready to fight and it didn't matter with whom. During the confusion, I took Lynn and went out the side door. Well the deck hand that worked for the guys I had punched out saw me go out the door and came outside. Solley's bouncer was right behind him, not to stop the fight, but to see that I had a fair fight. (I was a good customer) It was a quick fight and he went down hard and never moved. The bouncer told us to go on home and he dragged the man back into the nightclub.

Needless to say, this wasn't the way to make points with one's wife and there definitely weren't any midnight kisses after we got home. I apologized to Lynn once more before going to work.

I was sitting in my office thinking I wasn't any different than my step dad. I wasn't physically harming my wife, but mentally she was becoming a nervous wreck from my hot temper. This wasn't the first time she had seen me in fights, but the fifth or sixth time. The next day a policeman came to my office and questioned me about the fight. I told him just what I have written here.

He then explained to me that one man had a broken jaw and a brain concussion; the other man had four teeth that were damaged so badly they couldn't save them and a shattered cheekbone. The man that I knocked down outside and didn't move, also had a broken nose and brain concussion. His head had hit a rock when he went down in the parking lot that was all large gravel. He had been unconscious and had only woken up a few hours before the policeman came to see me. "You are a very lucky man," he said. Right now I wasn't feeling very lucky. "I could have been here to arrest you for murder, if he had died." I definitely didn't like the -died part and started getting nervous. "The only reason I'm not arresting you now," he went on "is because I talked to some people down at Solley's that saw the man follow you outside when you were trying to leave." (Solley didn't want to lose a good customer) "So, unless one of them presses charges against you, I will just put this report in my files. So you have a good day, Mr. Holbrook." He turned back and looked at me. "You are very highly respected in the community, sir. I hope you don't have any more trouble out of these men. He paused and said, "And I hope you don't visit Solley's too often."

The officers' words stuck with me the next couple of days. I finally had to take a good look at myself. I knew I had both a drinking and temper problem and I had better get both of them under control or lose my family or kill someone or both.

I loved my job, but I loved my family even more, so I decided it was time to leave Kodiak. I talked to my boss and told him I had made the decision to go back to Washington. They spent days trying to talk me out of it. Even the new dollar signs they waved at me didn't change my mind. I started breaking in a new man to take my place. In a month or so I drove the car with my family aboard the state ferry. This took us to Seward, Alaska and from there we drove down the Alaska Highway. We camped at parks and lakes and enjoyed seeing lots of wild life but mostly enjoyed being together as a family. I had a great time, even without one drink of alcohol.

I have wondered many times, when we push ourselves so hard, are we trying to prove that we are worthy? I know it was prideful and wrong, but it gave me a good feeling, when in Alaska, to hire school teachers, soon to be doctors, and lawyers that came there to work through the summer. I hope they went on to be very successful in life, but I had that selfish hour when they worked for me. "Look, Mama, look at me. See what a good boy I am, Mama."

CHAPTER 9

Back Home

We were back in Washington. Our place looked good to us as we pulled into the driveway. The kids quickly jumped out of the car and started playing in the big green field. The kids were happy and Lynn was all smiles again. She could drive to the grocery store on black top roads instead of dust and gravel. My family was all doing good and we once again had a get together at our mini farm.

We bought our first brand new car and still had enough money left to start a small logging company. As John said, "Fred finally struck gold in Alaska."

I got married to that logging company for the next few years. It saw much more of me than my family did. There isn't any way I can explain how hard it is for me to not be this way. I would take a Sunday off once or twice a month and devote the whole day to Lynn and the kids. It may have been as simple as a picnic down on the river where the kids could swim, play or just sit and talk to me about things that were important to them.

Our son, Rick, was definitely going to be the outdoor type. He loved going fishing and riding out on the logging roads with me. He is 48 years old as I write this and we still enjoy doing this.

As my income kept getting better and better, we sold the mini farm and moved to Central Park, a suburb of Aberdeen, Washington. I found my prestigious home, a beautiful tri level, three-bedroom, two-bath, with a family room big enough for a pool table, and was surrounded by wealthy people. I thought this was where I belonged, now with my bank account full and my prestigious home on the hill. I sure was proud of me.

CHAPTER 10

Family goes to Aberdeen

S hirley was married four times. It seemed like she was looking for the love she had never known as a child and was always searching for someone to fulfill her needs. I felt Red, her first husband, really loved and cared for her and the kids.

About this time in her life she came to the Lord. This seemed to fill the emptiness in her. Soon after this she met and married Blaine. He is a very quality man and proved this by standing by her and meeting her every need through three bypass surgeries plus other illnesses and I have a lot of respect for him. Shirley had gone to beauty school, and also owned and ran a restaurant for about a year but because of health problems had to give it up. She, like Wilma was a fabulous cook.

Wilma divorced Dan. A few years later she married Dave who owned a charter boat and together they bought a nice restaurant and nightclub and later a bowling alley. Things looked really good for awhile. They were off to Hawaii, Vegas and Reno. Life was good. Then the fishing industry in Westport collapsed and never recovered. It was totally dependant on the fishing industry and it became almost a ghost town overnight. They sold out and went to Louisiana where they bought a restaurant and nightclub.

They started having problems and sold the business. He took a job running boat for an oil company and Wilma came back to Washington and started a restaurant in Raymond. This restaurant burned and was mostly destroyed so she moved to Aberdeen where she started a prosperous catering business called, "A Touch of Class." Now, Wilma came to the Lord about this time, and devoted a lot of her time and skill cooking for the church she attended. She had a lot of physical problems, first having breast cancer, then an aneurysm, then later a heart attack. She got so she couldn't keep the business going because of a lot of back problems.

Jack had gone into the navy right out of high school and while stationed in San Diego, California, he met Dee, a girl from Idaho and married her. They had three kids; Chawnelle, Dawnelle and Deric. He was in aviation and traveled to many countries for the next twenty- eight years and didn't see his family as often as he would have liked to. He loved learning and spent hundreds of hours in school furthering his education and improving his chance of advancement.

Jerry, I think was only twenty years old when he started his own logging company. He had graduated from Ocosta High School and went to Grays Harbor College and studied engineering. About this time he married Penny. They had two sons, Jeff and Richie.

Things were tough the first couple of years. Jerry's youth and inexperience were overcome by persistence and long hard hours on the job. After about two years things turned around for Jerry and Penny and they built a nice big home on some acreage. Jerry's vision was always bigger than mine. On second thought, I think our vision was about the same, but Jerry was much bolder about going after that dream.

Jerry built another big home and also a grocery store with a deli in it. Penny ran this at the same time they bought another logging company. Now remember, this was the young couple in their early twenties. Then things changed overnight. This was in the seventies when interest rates went from eight percent to twenty two percent within a few months. This put a slump in the housing market therefore causing the timber industry to crash.

Now they were making payments on three homes, a grocery store and two logging companies and no market for any of it. In time they used up their resources while hoping for a turn around that didn't come and they finally had to file for bankruptcy.

Now there is one thing I want to get across in this book, and that's the choices we have in life. Jerry could have given up. There were lots of things he could have blamed for his bad luck, but instead they chose to go back to work, Jerry for a log exporter and Penny for the County Health Department.

After a year or so Jerry went to work managing a logging company and after a year bought the company and set up an export yard in Olympia, Washington, exporting mostly to the Chinese.

I've spent less time with Ginny than with any of the other kids. She was born after I left home and I was only around her for a few months the first eleven years of her life. After mom died, Ginny lived with Wilma until she graduated from High School. Then following a trend, like the other girls, she went to beauty school in Olympia. While there she met and married Russ. He was in the army at Ft. Lewis, Washington and after his time in the army was up, they moved to Missoula, Montana, where he was from. She had two kids with Russ, Shelly and Rusty. They divorced after awhile and she and the kids moved back to Raymond, Washington and soon she began working in a beauty shop in Aberdeen.

Chuck tried a lot of different businesses. He had a vending machine route, pinball machines, and a poolroom. It was around this time he met and married Elva Lynn. She was a waitress in a restaurant and had two kids by a former marriage. They later had a son, Zane.

Now Chuck needed a more positive income, so they moved to Aberdeen where he started driving logging truck for Weyerhaeuser Timber Co. They bought a home in Central Park. Elva Lynn went to beauty school and Chuck went to real estate school at night and they both got their license. They converted one of the rooms in the basement into a beauty shop and Elva was soon working long hours fixing hair. Chuck was selling real estate evenings after driving truck all day.

John, like the rest of us wanted his own business. Opal had now spent a number of years working in a restaurant and one day a couple came in from eastern Washington to have some tires repaired. They mentioned that they owned a restaurant and was getting ready to sell it. John and Opal had talked about opening a restaurant of their own for quite awhile, but were never able to find the right place. They made an appointment with the people to look at the restaurant the following weekend. After they got there, they felt it was perfect because it was a nice restaurant and that included a nice home next door. They worked out a contract on the spot and right then became restaurateurs. They put their home on the market and gave notice to their employers and soon had a very prosperous restaurant going.

It wasn't a big surprise when three years later I got the news that John and Opal had split up. If you can believe it, John was far more hot-headed than I was. His family never knew what might send him into a rage. It could be as simple a thing as Opal would forget to wash his work clothes. He might throw the washing machine out in the yard and maybe the dryer, too. This caused his family to spend a lot of years walking on tiptoes.

After three years working together in the restaurant, it finally came to a head and Opal filed for divorce. John moved back to a small town thirty miles from me and went to work once again for a large tire company. About a year later he met Terri, a quality lady with two small boys from a previous marriage and they got married. John's two youngest kids, Rocky and Barbara came to live with him.

Evelyn was the last one to come to Washington. This completed our migration. Once again we were altogether. We had a bunch of good times together and had a family reunion every year so all the younger generation could get better acquainted with each other.

Remember she had gotten married to Clyde just after the bad year we had on the Virginia farm. She had taken her daughter Phyllis and moved with Clyde to Michigan. Well, a short time after I left Michigan, Clyde died from T.B. After a time she married Gene Taylor and they had three kids, Robert, Betty and Connie.

Evelyn wasn't the aggressive type, but she had always dreamed of having a story book house sitting on a knoll with a white picket fence, a swing on the front porch and flowers growing along the walk way. Her oldest daughter Phyllis was working in a pizza place back east and Evelyn felt she could put in her own pizza place and make a lot of money. Only one problem, they didn't have any money. I did some research and found out pizza places were really getting popular back east, but hadn't gotten started in the Northwest.

Now they were living with Lynn and I. Gene as yet didn't have a job, so they didn't meet any of the requirements for a bank loan. I was making more money than I ever thought possible so we loaned them the ten thousand dollars to frame the restaurant, and put a three- bedroom apartment overhead. I then went to the bank and co-signed for the remainder of the loan to finish the building. They were soon ready to open the doors of their new restaurant in a good location in Westport, close to Wilma's motel.

Now about this time brother Jerry had a logging company, I had a logging company, Chuck was in the real estate business, we were all building houses, the girls were getting paid for rolling peoples hair in little bundles, then sending them out to eat in their restaurants, and Jack was flying around the world in Navy jets making our borders safe for us. How good can it get?

CHAPTER 11

Dark Clouds on the Horizon

B ut there were dark clouds on the horizon. I was out on the job one day and started having chest pain. After a few weeks of this I went to the Dr. and he checked me out. He asked me how old I was. "I'm thirty six," I told him. He asked me if there were any heart problems in my family. "My dad died of a heart attack at the age of thirty eight," I told him "and my Mom at age forty seven."

"I'm going to give you a prescription for nitroglycerin. When you get this chest pain, put one under your tongue and if the pain consistently goes away, you come back and see me." I was familiar with the nitro pills. I had seen my Dad take them in the months before he died.

I felt lower than the vest buttons on a caterpillar for the next couple weeks. The stress from thinking I might have problems like my Dad, was heavy on my mind. This may have been the reason for the increased pain in my chest for the next three weeks. Practically any activity brought on chest pain. The nitro seemed to help, but left me with a headache.

Over the next couple months I went through a bunch of tests. Finally the Dr. sent me to Seattle. They kept me in there two or three days running tests. Finally my heart Dr. and the surgeons came into my room, closed the door, pulled up chairs and started explaining to us what the tests had shown. I had very severe artery disease and my arteries were almost totally closed off. They felt if they did bypass surgery, which was brand new in 1970, that I would probably die on the operating table and worse yet that I might have maybe only about six months to live. This would give time to get my life in order. No more strenuous work and not even watch a football game if it excited me. Lynn later told me that I had turned chalky white when I heard the verdict.

There was an unusual quietness as Lynn drove the eighty miles back to our home in Aberdeen. We were both in shock, too much so to talk. I laid my head back and closed my eyes. I was still having trouble accepting the diagnosis. I was a fairly heavy smoker, a pack a day. I had quit drinking about four years earlier. I was in perfect physical condition from climbing up and down mountains while logging. I ran heavy equipment and less than a year before, I could throw a two hundred pound elk quarter on my back and carry it out of the woods without any problem. It had always been important for me to stay tough and stout.

I looked over at Lynn and I could see she was having her own struggles. She had never worked outside the home and was very content just being a good housewife and mother. I took care of all the business problems and paid all the bills. Now if I died she was going to be left with a logging company she knew nothing about, plus properties scattered around the harbor. This caused my mind to wander back in time. I could see the fear in my Mother's face when my Dad died, and Mom was wondering how she was going to run a business and raise seven kids.

A few days after we got back from Seattle, we loaded up the kids and went on a picnic. I had bought a twenty-two acre parcel of land with merchantable timber on it a month or so earlier, about twenty miles from our house. I wanted to go look it over and maybe resell it. There was a two-acre field in back of the timber and we walked back to it and had our picnic. The kids had also been under a lot of pressure and they were like young colts let out of the barn. They ran and hollered and climbed trees until they wore themselves out. I sat there looking around and thought "what a beautiful place to build a home." The kids had never liked our prestigious home in town. Before, we had always had a home with big lots or acreage.

I had also bought eighty acres about six months before that had a lake on it. I had thought about building a house on it but had trouble getting permits. The lake ran into a popular river and fish went into it to spawn, so the state fisheries were holding it up.

It had now gotten hard for me to climb the stairs in our tri-level home. As I sat there watching the kids play, I thought, "I can spend my last days laying on a couch or I can go out with style." So the next day I brought my equipment out and starting building a road through the timber back to the field. I made a nice circle driveway about a quarter of a mile long.

A couple of days later we were in Olympia, shopping and drove by a Mobile Home Sales. They had a double wide on display that caught our eye. I wheeled in, attracted to the outside appearance. I had never been inside a double wide before and was curious to see if the inside matched the quality of the outside's three tab roof and beveled aluminum siding. We were impressed with the kitchens and bathrooms. They were well done and had copper plumbing and Moen faucets. The salesman gave us a price that was quite high and some literature. We crossed the street to a restaurant and while having lunch, talked about having the factory built home put on our new home site and later build a home next to it, then sell or rent the double wide. By doing this we could be moved in within a month or two.

We went back to the dealer and negotiated a price. They wanted to keep it there for a showplace for the next six weeks, which we were agreeable to. This would give me time to get cement work done for the home.

It was a happy day when we moved into our sixteen hundred square foot factory built home. I had never seen the kids so excited. The next few months taught me a valuable lesson. Happiness isn't found in prestige houses, big bank accounts, shiny new cars, or diamonds and silk cloth. Happiness is having peace within. It comes when we can accept who we are inside and are willing to trade worldly wealth for quiet time with your wife. It's when you relax before a fireplace while rocking a child that you have helped bring into the world and let the sound of his rhythmic breathing bring peace to one's soul. It comes when you walk hand in hand with your five and six year olds, while the sun is dropping behind the evergreen trees, and you don't feel rushed when you stop and watch the hard working ants drag cuttings of cherry tree leaves. He doesn't seem to know where home is. The leaf is much bigger than he is, but he wants it all. I had spent much of my life like the little ant.

CHAPTER 12

A Friendly Town

The small town of Elma, a population of about three thousand, was very friendly, and we soon had people dropping in to wish us well. A man that I respected stopped in one morning and told me that the talk of the town was about an Evangelist that had a healing ministry and was having meetings at a local church. There were people by the dozens getting healed. They were getting out of wheelchairs and walking. He had been there the night before and didn't think there was anything fake about it. He was hoping I would go see if I could get healed. When I thought about it through the day, I was struggling with "if there really is a God, then where was He when we were small kids and were sleeping in barn lofts and coal mines?" Now my neighbor was telling me God was just a few minutes away where He was doing miracles through an Evangelist.

I had a man overseeing my logging company as it was getting harder to get out of the house and do things, so; I thought "what have I got to lose?" Lynn had heard the conversation and got hyped up. So we showed up at the church with people lined up to get in and we had to sit in the back row, which was fine with me. After a few songs, the evangelist got up and spoke for a while. He was a good speaker and seemed sure of himself. Then he called for anyone who wanted to be healed to come forward.

A logger friend I knew, with busted up legs from a tractor rolling over him, stood upon his crutches and went up. The evangelist took his crutches and broke them. This got my undivided attention. He then prayed for the man and to my amazement, my friend walked off the platform without a limp. This type of thing went on for an hour. I came out impressed with what I saw happen. I didn't go up for prayer, but decided to go back the next night.

When we entered the church, I had already made up my mind, if he asked for people to come and be prayed for I was going to go up. The service started with people giving testimony of being healed from just about everything one could think of. When he called for the sick and the lame, I went forward with about fifty others. I saw people that were practically deaf get their hearing back. I saw a person wearing glasses as thick as a coke bottle prayed for and read fine print without their glasses. When it was my turn, he asked me if I was a Christian. I said, "No" so he asked me to pray the words he said. I repeated them then he prayed for my heart trouble. I didn't feel any change in my body so he told me to believe and accept the healing. So I left the church feeling good. Lynn had gone up and committed her life to the Lord and we were up for hours all excited about our new experience.

The next day I got up and went out on the job. I was walking over some of the ground my crew had logged to see what kind of job they had been doing because I had high logging standards. I very quickly realized my heart problem was still there and there was no healing. I remember Lynn talking about feeling saved and clean inside. I sat down on a stump and looked out over a canyon, as a soft breeze carried the sound of the big engine of my equipment to my ears.

I thought this might be the last time I will ever hear that sound. I felt lonely and scared. I wondered, out of all the miracles last night, why wasn't I one of them? As I thought back on last night, I realized that when I went forward, it was for a physical healing, but if I got a spiritual healing, that also would have been all right. But what I really wanted was a physical healing.

I became very depressed, to the point of giving up. I wondered what was wrong with me that my Mom didn't want me and now God didn't want me. I sat down and felt sorry for myself for a few minutes and then there was a peace that came over me. I started thinking about how blessed I was in so many ways. I had a beautiful loving wife, four beautiful children, and my brothers and sisters were all back together, so I drove back home with a fairly good feeling.

The next day I bought a Bible and started reading it, but had a hard time understanding it. We started going to the church where we had attended the crusade. Lynn seemed to be more fulfilled in her life but I was still having doubts. One day a logger friend stopped by and was telling me that he had heard the Virginia Mason Hospital in Seattle was having great success in doing bypass surgeries.

After my friend left, I had mixed emotions. I wanted to live, but I didn't think I could stand another rejection. Maybe it was time to let happen what would happen and quit worrying about it.

CHAPTER 13

Decision Time Again

Once again it was decision time. I walked over and looked out the picture window. It was the last week in April. I had just gotten the circle drive blacktopped and it looked shiny and clean. The fir trees were putting on new growth and the light green against the older dark green showed the amount of growth. I had planted Rhododendrons under the trees, with the native ferns and their pink and white blooms were starting to show. I also had planted flowering Japanese cherry trees on the lawn side of the circle drive and they were in bloom. There had been a light rain a few hours earlier and everything looked so lush and beautiful. Everywhere I looked there was new growth, new life flowing through God's creation. I remembered reading in my new Bible that morning in Ecclesiastes 3:

> "To everything there is a season,
>   a time for everything under the heaven:
> A time to be born and a time to die;
>   a time to plant, and a time to pluck up
> What is planted; a time to kill,
>   a time to heal.

A time to break down,
   And a time to build up;
A time to weep and a time to laugh;
   A time to Mourn; and a time to dance."
(NKJ Spirit Filled Life Bible)

   I told Lynn to call and make an appointment with Virginia Mason. Well, I did go to Seattle and had a quadruple bypass. I hardly had any trouble recovering and in about six weeks was back into my twelve hour a day work habit.

   I wanted to spend more time with my family, so we bought a new motor home and managed to get in a few short journeys and some camping and also spent a day now and then on the river fishing.

   Over the years, my son Rick and I learned where all the wild life and fish lived and we managed to bring home more than our share. I still remember with pleasure those days spent in the outdoors with my son, and later my grandsons.

   About a year after my bypass surgery, I started thinking of ways to stimulate a good income in case this should happen again, something that Lynn and the kids could manage. I decided on a mobile home park. I logged and cleared fifteen of the twenty-two acres where our home was and after a few months of working with the planning department, I'd gotten approval for sixty- five spaces. I had my own equipment to do the work and enjoyed the challenge. It was a pleasure to be able to do physical work again. I soon had Phase 1 black-topped and ready but this was new territory for me and had no way of knowing how fast the spaces would fill up. I knew I had a very quality park, and to my surprise the homes started coming in faster than I could build carports. This soon generated a very nice income. I felt comfortable now, that if something happened to me, Lynn and the kids would be well taken care of.

Life went on pretty normal for a time but we would later find out that none of my family would escape the inherited curse of high cholesterol and coronary artery disease.

A year after my surgery, John had to go through the same ordeal, and within the next five years, Evelyn, Chuck, and Shirley would get their turn at bypass surgery. Too bad we hadn't taken out stock at Virginia Mason. Over the years the doctors became like family to us.

I was visiting with John in his room just before his surgery. We were talking about old times and remembering the time when one autumn day I was laying in front of my fireplace dozing, when John came by. He said he had a good idea, "What's that?" I asked.

"Well, it's a month until elk season," he said.

"I know and I'm looking forward to it," I said.

"Well, what I've been thinking is, why spend all that money chasing those elk up and down the mountain side and wearing out our bodies and our truck, when for less money we could go to the Chehalis County Auction and buy a good grain fed beef, bring it home and butcher it. We could hang it in your shed for a few days and we would have four or five hundred pounds of prime beef." I sat up from my warm mat and looked at John. "I thought that would interest you," John said. The reason I sat up was from remembering last year just before hunting season John and I were sitting in my boat fishing, when he came up with the thought of going to the auction and buying a hog.

We laughed about that for years because the old sow was so tough, every time we tried to fry it, the meat would just turn up in the frying pan, so we had to make it all into sausage. Now a year later John was telling me about cheap prime rib and T-bone steaks.

Well, my mini farm was fenced and I had been thinking about buying a couple yearlings and letting them put on three or four hundred pounds; butcher one and sell the other. "Why go to all the time and trouble of feeding and caring for them when we can go to the auction and buy an eight hundred pound steer for a few dollars each and in a week or so, we can be eating prime rib?"

In a couple hours we had a cattle rack on my half ton pickup and were on our way to the auction. I was hoping to go home with a nice white face or a black angus.

There was a lot of bidding and the beef was going higher than normal. It didn't look like they were going to be much cheaper than the elk. Then out of the chute came this cross-bred long horn, a thousand pounds of him. He charged the two men in the arena, his head lowered with those fifteen inch horns flashing. The men wisely scaled the heavy board fence, not a second too soon. Everyone was having a good laugh as the big steer tried to find an exit or make a new one. "Now don't let them horns get your attention off the fact that this is as good a beef as any that's went through here today," said the auctioneer. "It's probably some little grandma's pet and it's just upset. Why, she probably hand fed it three times a day. Just look at that flat back. Why, there is a ton of steaks under that hide. Now who will start the bid at two hundred?"

"Here, said John.

"I need two twenty five."

"Here" said a woman from the back row.

"Why it's a little lady wanting to take him home for her kids to play with. Now, who will give me...?"

"Here" said John.

"Let her buy him" I said to John. "I have seen bull elk tamer than that walleyed thing."

"Fred, it's just scared. It doesn't make him any less a good animal."

"Going once, going twice, sold!" said the auctioneer, just as the long horn tried to crawl over that eight-foot board fence. I thought for a minute he was going to make it.

"What in the world have we done, John and how are we going to keep that beast from tearing up my truck?"

"We will tie his horns to the cattle rack and once we get going he will be so busy trying to keep his balance, he won't have time to worry about getting out," John said.

"This sure isn't as much fun as elk hunting," I said. "I wish I had brought my elk gun. I'm afraid we might need it."

When I backed up to the loading shoot, about half a dozen men came wandering over to watch the excitement. I had lots of rope and we decided to double it for safety. We gave the gatekeeper our paperwork. "Are you the ones that bought the cross breed with the horns?" he asked.

"That's us," I said.

"I'll run him into the loading chute and my job is done," he said. John and I were both nervous, but to our surprise, the steer was pretty calm. John reached into the chute and stroked him a few times. The steer looked much bigger than a thousand pounds. We slipped a couple loops over his horns. Then the fun began. We were all wringing wet with sweat, by the time we got him anchored to the pickup. I think half the community evacuated until we left town, half an hour later.

We had a thirty- mile trip to home and that beast fought all the way. The two by six sideboards were like stove wood and the back window got busted out. I thought a couple of times he was going to crawl through it.

We finally made it home. I wanted to shoot the thing, but we backed the truck out into the field, cut the rope, and jumped back in the truck. He jumped out and walked about fifty feet and started munching grass like it was no big deal. John and I were still shaking hours later. But we got the last laugh about a week later when we turned him into steaks and the prime rib was delicious.

After John had recuperated from his surgery and felt good enough to get outdoors again, we spent quite a bit of time hiking into the high country and fishing the lakes. We would spend a day or two all alone and John felt comfortable talking to me about the Lord.

I was six years older than Chuck, but was gone through most of his growing up years. We had different interests. I liked to hunt and fish, but Chuck had no interest in any of that. But we did enjoy working the real estate market together and both kept our eyes open for that good deal that occasionally comes by.

Chuck was always the center of attention at the party each year at our family picnic. He liked to laugh and always had a funny story to tell. Wilma and Chuck became very close and shared their restaurant knowledge. Wilma enjoyed cooking big special meals for him and he had a gourmet taste that kept him about twenty pounds overweight.

He had bought up a number of houses and apartments and had owned three different restaurants. Elva Lynn closed the beauty shop and spent long hours working the restaurants.

Chuck never quit looking for that perfect spot to start one more business.

CHAPTER 14

My Trip down the River

Well, I had been encouraging Lynn to be all she could be, but the most helpful thing for her came through the church. She had a good musical voice and started leading the worship service and teaching ladies Bible Study and went on to become the Sunday School Superintendent. By this time I was only going to church when there was some special thing going on and Lynn would encourage me to attend. I felt our Pastor was a good teacher of the Word, but a boring preacher and I used this excuse not to attend church. By now I was trying to buy my way into heaven. If the church needed anything, all they had to do was say the word and I would pay the lion's share, new pews, new carpet, intercoms, piano, etc.

I was starting to have lots of chest pain again. I was on a lot of heart medication along with blood thinners, but nothing seemed to stop that inherited cholesterol problem that had become a plague to my family.

One early morning I was sitting in my boat enjoying my favorite thing, fishing for silver salmon. I had a nice fifteen pound one in the boat and a nice one on my line, when I started having chest pain. I managed to get my bottle of nitro, which I now carried all the time. I put one under my tongue and this usually gave me quick relief, but this morning the pain seemed to get worse. I stuck another nitro in my mouth and realized I was smoking a cigarette, which I threw away, but the pain kept getting worse. I was getting very concerned, even to cutting the line and letting the fish go. My head was now throbbing and I could hardly breathe from all the pain. There were bench seats in the boat, so I lay down while trying to get another nitro out of the bottle. They spilled onto the floor of the wet boat. I laid there looking up at the dark, overcast sky and then the boat started going around and I felt myself being pulled down. It was like the swirl of water going down a drain and I felt like I was pulled down through this tunnel, into a dark dreary place. I tried to scream out but there was no sound and there was no light. I can't explain how dark it was. No sound, no light and no air. It was a place of nothingness, a place of no hope. I realized it was a place without God.

I had a forty-foot redwood log fall on me when I was a young man, and it looked like I might die, but I still had hope. I have hunted all over the Northwest, including Canada and Alaska and have been lost, but felt I could make it out.

Once I was hunting in Montana, just outside of West Yellowstone. It was a guided hunt. We rode horses back to the ten thousand-foot elevations before daylight. There was about six inches of fresh snow on the ground. Now I was supposed to hunt on foot up over this mountain and down into the next basin where the guide was going to be waiting for me with the horses.

A client had killed an elk the evening before and the guide was going to load the elk onto a couple of horses and go back to camp. While loading the elk the guide had gotten a broken leg because the horse got spooked and came over backwards. Now the guide that was going to meet me some miles away had to get the man with the broken leg to the hospital. If this wasn't enough, a blizzard blew in with heavy winds and snowing so hard I could only see a few feet in front of me.

By the time I got to where I thought he was going to meet me, there was over a foot of snow. Now, not finding the guide and no let up in the snow, I was becoming concerned. My lunch and survival gear was on the horse that was no longer with me. I didn't have the foggiest idea of how to get back to camp. He was supposed to be there by noon.

I waited until two o'clock and then made the decision to back track myself in hopes I could recognize some landmarks that I had purposely noticed. It wasn't long until my tracks weren't visible anymore. The snow was two feet deep and my body was tiring fast. I had no food and had been hiking since daylight. In another couple hours it would be dark.

I began thinking maybe this is where I would meet my waterloo. I was so sweaty and wet from the snow, I felt like I would freeze to death if I stopped moving. It was a thirty-mile an hour wind, and icy cold. Well, this wasn't a very good position to be in. But I still had hope. There was still life all around me. I could hear and see the wind and still see and feel the snow. I still felt like I was going to make it out of there alive.

But this place of darkness and nothingness made me realize there is a God and now I was separated from Him. Now I knew He was with me when the car stopped short of going over the one hundred foot cliff. He was there when the rifle didn't fire and the One who kept the nail from penetrating Woody's brain instead of the wall. I now knew He was there when I looked out my picture window and saw the beauty of His handiwork. He was the One that placed the good thoughts in my mind. He was in the soft breeze that brought the sounds from my equipment to my ears and the One that brought comfort to my heart when I was about to give up.

I cried out with the voice of my spirit and told God how sorry I was for doubting His existence and begged Him to take me out of this pit and if He would, I would never again have any doubts of whom He was. With these words, I started back up through that tunnel. I awoke still lying on the boat seat. When I had lain down in the boat, the sky was dark and cloudy. Now when I opened my eyes, the clouds had moved back, letting the sun shine through them and the moisture in the air caused the sun's rays to sparkle, and it seemed to deliberately shine it's rays of warmth into my body.

I sat up very tired, but alive. I picked up my pack of cigarettes and threw them into the river and watched the river carry them away. I knew I would never smoke another cigarette. I needed a new physical heart but God gave me a new spiritual heart that day. The old heart was filled with pride, selfishness, greed, lust, hate and many other things I don't even know about. In return he gave me a heart that can feel the needs and hurts of other people.

I left the river that day a changed man, not physically, but spiritually. I went home to be a better husband to my wife and spend more time with my kids. One of the most amazing things to me is, when I started reading the Bible it started coming alive and I began to understand it. The sermons of the Pastor that earlier I had found so boring, I now found my self enjoying. I later become an elder in that church.

CHAPTER 15

Another Change for Evelyn

My Sister Evelyn's troubles were still not over. Like John and Opal a few years earlier, she and Gene started having marital problems. They too were spending twenty- four hours a day working with each other. Their daughter Connie was a very intelligent girl with more common sense than her mother or father and was going to school and still working long hours at the restaurant. It all came to a head when Gene filed for divorce, packed his bags and went back to Ohio.

The restaurant was in the town of Westport where there was now a depression in the fishing industry. Westport had been a party town and people came from all over the U.S. to fish and party, often more partying than fishing. There were lots of nightclubs and most had live music nightly and it was easy to get caught up in the excitement. Evelyn and Wilma both had gotten caught up in the flow of the tide. This could have been the reason for Evelyn's loss of husband and business when the fishing industry collapsed.

One day I got a call Evelyn was going to file for bankruptcy and was leaving town. If you remember I had co-signed a note for the bank loan to finish the restaurant. Just that quick,

I inherited a huge debt of a restaurant I didn't want. The place had gotten kind of run down and the upstairs apartment was never finished.

I knew nothing about restaurants, so I called my brother Chuck, who had now become a restaurateur and a real estate broker. He looked it over along with the prospects of recovery for that town and felt it wasn't that good. We were both good carpenters and we felt the best thing was to finish everything up. So we got our hammers and saws and spent about a month finishing it up getting it ready to market. Chuck put it on the market, advertising heavily in the Seattle area and found a buyer for it. We both came out making a few dollars.

Sometimes owning your own business can be a curse, especially when it destroys families. Evelyn had left the area for a few months and then moved back to Raymond. I stopped by to see her and she was still drinking and appeared to be very uncomfortable around me and kept apologizing for sticking me with the restaurant. I told her it was all right, that I hadn't lost any money on it. I told her about my trip down the river and how the Lord had taken the worry over money from me. Lynn and I prayed often for Evelyn and we stopped by to encourage her from time to time.

One day she stopped by our place with a man she had started dating. His name was Ray Carlson. I liked him right off. He was calm, intelligent and was very gentle and patient with her. I was glad when a few months later they got married. The next couple of years were very happy for Evelyn. She stopped drinking. Ray treated her like she always wanted to be treated.

Isn't it something how quick one's life can be turned around? One early morning Ray was going to the grocery store and while crossing the railroad tracks was hit and killed by a train. This devastated Evelyn so much she didn't want to live and got to the point for weeks, she didn't want to see anyone. But the family was faithful to go by often and let her know we all loved her. Shortly after this she had to have bypass surgery and came through it, but wasn't ever able to be very active after that.

One late summer day, she and her daughter Phyllis came by. We were happy to see them and went out to greet them. We had chairs sitting under the shade trees, and they wanted to sit outside. It had been a long time since I had seen her look so good. She didn't have that drawn and bitter look that I remembered the last time I had seen her. I commented on how good she looked and kidded her about having a new boyfriend in her life. "It's better than that, brother." She said. "I found Jesus." I was so shocked I just about fell off my chair. She went on to say, that about a month before, she had started thinking about the difference in her life and mine and saw the happiness in Lynn and I since we had become Christians. One morning she got on her knees and cried out to God and asked Him to take away this heavy burden she had been carrying. "I actually felt this peace come over me and it got better as the day went on," she said. "I even threw my cigarettes in the garbage and haven't smoked one since." Lynn and I prayed with them before they left and I have never had a better feeling about someone's salvation.

A week later, we got a call from Phyllis that Evelyn had been taken by helicopter to Virginia Mason Hospital with a severe heart attack. Lynn and I got there as soon as possible. They had already started surgery. She had been about five hours in surgery when Dr. Paul came out to the waiting room where all the family was now gathered. She had made it through the surgery and was in Intensive Care, but things didn't look very good as her heart had been severely damaged and the next few hours as always, were very critical. As I stood there in the intensive care room, looking down at Evelyn, and listening to the machines that was keeping life pumped into her body, my mind went back over the years as I remembered the tragedies in her life.

Her first husband had walked out on her before Phyllis was born, her second husband Clyde died of T.B., Gene, her third husband and the father of her children, was electrocuted shortly after they divorced while doing maintenance work on a swimming pool, Bob, her only son, was born with a defective heart valve and had to have surgery when he was four months old, and as a result had brain damage and was always mentally five or six years behind others his age. She spent her life devoted to looking for hospitals that could help Bob, but to no avail.

When her daughter Betty Ann was four years old, they were on the freeway and had a collision with a semi truck. Evelyn grabbed Betty Ann in her arms as they crashed. The car went into a spin, throwing them out of the car onto the highway. The wheels of the semi came down and severed the head of the baby. Evelyn had broken legs, a crushed pelvis, broken ribs, punctured lung, a broken jaw and a brain concussion. I cringe as I tell this.

It was many months and many trips back to the doctors, but her body finally did heal yet her mind was always tormented and kept reliving the accident. She would wake up screaming, as her mind would over and over relive that awful scene. But time has that magic way of making our hurts and pains become distant. It's almost like it wasn't you, but like it happened to someone else. This must be God's way of helping us heal.

Evelyn died a couple days after the heart surgery with family by her side. I remember looking down at her swollen body, thinking it didn't at all resemble my sister.

When I think of her now, I see her sitting under the shade tree, drinking iced tea, with a smile on her face and a twinkle in her eyes and hear the words "I have found something better, I have found Jesus." I hope her mansion on the hill exceeds all her expectations.

CHAPTER 16

My Second Heart Surgery

July of 1986 was once again decision time. I was having so much chest pain I had to sleep sitting up and just walking through the house would cause angina. I now had most everything in order for my family's future income.

One morning I told Lynn that I was going to have bypass surgery again, even though my cardiologist was against it. This upset Lynn but even though she questioned my decision, it was for me to decide, and she didn't try to talk me out of it. She knew what a hard decision it was for me to make.

The first day of August, I once again went under the knife. The next nine days were a nightmare for Lynn, my kids and the rest of my family. I had been unconscious for eight of those days. My body had shut down and they had me on life support equipment with tubes and lines going every which way. I had swollen so much they couldn't even sew my chest back together and were afraid of infection.

On the ninth day I woke up and saw Lynn sitting there. I tried smiling at her, but they had a tube in my throat and my mouth was taped. My eyes were probably so blood shot I could imagine they probably looked like two olives in a glass of tomato juice. Lynn looked at me, smiled, and reached over and touched my arm and I knew everything was going to be all right.

I had no idea of the horror she had been through the past few days. My body started recovering fairly quickly, but I was having trouble concentrating on things. I also noticed I was having trouble reading. I mentioned this to the Dr and he said my body had been through a great ordeal and it would be a few days before things got back to normal.

It is now years later and normal has never yet happened. I literally had to learn to read all over again by watching Sesame Street with my grandchildren. I still struggle with writing, but I do fairly well with printing and my math is a disaster. I don't type, so this book was done first by my printing it by hand. Poor Lynn, she has to decipher my spelling and then type it up.

It sounds like I'm complaining, but I'm not. We've had a fantastic life and for the last thirty years we have been very involved in the Lord's work. We have attended three churches over the years and were elders in all three churches, thus giving us the privilege of teaching and ministering in many different ways, including visiting hospitals and praying for the sick. Who better would be suited for this ministry?

Our most rewarding years were spent dividing our time between our homes and churches in Washington and Lake Havasu City, Arizona. God had blessed us with the finances to afford a furnished home in both places. This gave us the chance to be with our children and grandchildren.

I can't possibly explain how blessed I feel by having those extra thirty plus years with my family. Lynn was able to be with our daughters when they gave birth to eight of our thirteen grandchildren. What a joy that was for her to be able to see new life brought into the world.

Our daughter Connie, as a young girl set her eyes on Jesus. She has a bachelor's degree in teaching and is at this writing, using her talent teaching and ministering at the Dream Center in Los Angeles, reaching out to the hurting young people and trying to bring some direction to their lives.

Our son Rick took after me in a lot of ways. He became a logger, falling timber and is still content doing that. He loves the outdoors. I would call him a survivor. Drop him off on the top of Mt. Rainier at night with a pocketknife and a few matches and by noon the following day he would have a lean to built and eating venison steaks, smothered in Chandelle mushrooms and wild blueberry pie for dessert.

Debbie is "miss super mom." She managed a career in dentistry and was still a good mother, never missing a Little League game or forgetting a birthday, always showing up for special events the kids were involved in. She was up late at night making cookies and fudge, cuddling and reading to the kids and up again at five the next morning.

Judy, like her mother chose to be a stay at home mom until her kids got older. She would have been a topnotch real estate lady, but she later chose restaurant work. She has had managerial training and is hoping to have her own restaurant in the near future.

Now as I finish the last pages of this book, Lynn and I are living in our modest twenty two hundred square foot home in Sun City West, Arizona. We have sold our home in Washington because of my age and bad health, and will only be going back for a month or two in the summer to spend time with our kids, grandkids, and other family and friends.

EPILOGUE

Evelyn died after her second bypass surgery at the age of fifty seven.

John lived ten years after his bypass surgery. He died of a heart attack at the age of forty seven one day while changing a truck tire at the place where he worked.

Chuck lived 14 years after his bypass surgery. One day while repairing a roof on one of his rentals, he had a massive heart attack and died at the age of fifty seven.

Shirley went through three bypass surgeries and many other major problems. Her heart just couldn't take any more stress and at the age of sixty three died of a heart attack.

Living near me in Sun City West, Arizona is my sister Wilma. She has had a lot of physical problems the past couple of years. At the age of seventy one she still had the desire to work and worked at Sam's Club for about a year until she had to quit because of back and other health problems. She now stays home and mothers her cat, Missy.

Jack and Dee are now living in Las Vegas, Nevada and have purchased their second four hundred thousand dollar home. After twenty eight years in the Navy, he retired and went back to Washington for a few years, got his real estate and appraisers' license, and was overseeing the home building and sales for our brother Jerry. But Jack's heart was in aviation. A job for the FAA became available; he applied for and got the job. He's happy once again flying around the country as a Federal Aviation Inspector.

Jerry and Penny are still going full steam ahead. The logging company has expanded and he's still developing property and building houses. The last couple of years he has been investing in apartment houses and duplexes as rentals. Penny has a new adventure going, with Alpaca farming. She is well suited for this job because of her love for animals. At this time they are content living in their one point seven million dollar home on a lake in Olympia, Washington.

Ginny is a lot like Shirley was in her disposition, always being there to help someone in need. She always puts herself last. Life hasn't been too kind to her, either. Her son, Rusty, in his early twenties, died in the state of Texas. This hurt Ginny deeply and troubled her for a long time. One night as she was on her way to a family get together, a car rear ended her, giving her a severe whiplash, bothering her so badly, she had to give up her job as a beautician. The whiplash still bothers her to this day. She is living in the Portland, Oregon area close to her oldest daughter.

Woody died of lung cancer at the age of seventy seven.

Our family remains in close contact with each other.

I know bragging is tacky, and that is not my intention to do so, but it is to show the plateau my family has reached in life considering the start we had and the odds that were against us. Even as a dysfunctional family, it is up to each individual to choose the direction they go in life. The choices we make can come back as a blessing or come back to haunt you.

Joshua 24:15

"Choose ye this day whom you will serve,
but as for me and my house,
We will serve the Lord."
(NKJ Spirit Filled Life Bible)

Printed in the United States
72206LV00003B/2

9 781600 348860